Song of the Bessarabian Germans

Blessed be thou, my native land
God shed on thee His grace
The land where still my cradle stands
My father's chosen place.

A land so full of riches rife
I lock thee in my heart;
I will be true to thee in life
E'en death cannot us part.

Defend, O God, in joy and grief
Our precious native land
From fields with golden wheaten sheaves
To Black Sea's pearly strand.

God help us our fate to endure
Then with our fathers rest
O keep us German still and pure
In Motherland's safe breast.

—composed by Albert Mauch, 1922
translated by Nancy Bernhardt Holland, 1991

Copyright by Heimatbuch der Deutschen aus Bessarabien

IMMANUEL'S LIFE IN EUROPE 1916-1952

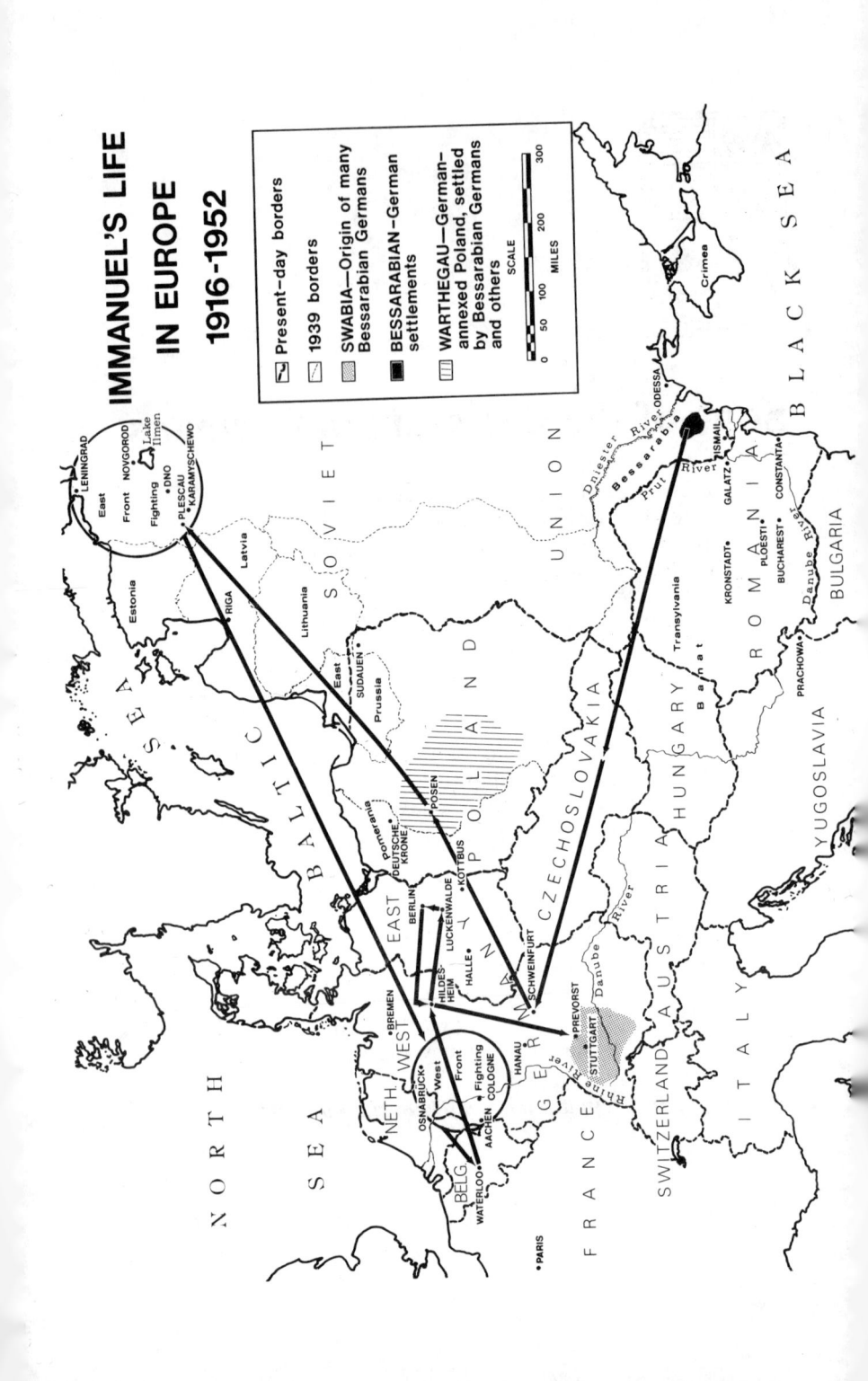

Bessarabian Knight

A Peasant Caught between the
Red Star and the Swastika

Immanuel Weiss's True Story

by

George F. Wieland

Published under the auspices of the
American Historical Society of Germans from Russia
631 D Street, Lincoln, Nebraska 68502-1199

Copyright © 1991 by George F. Wieland

Printed by
Augstums Printing Service, Inc.
Lincoln, Nebraska

Table of Contents

Introduction i

Chapter 1: Bessarabia 1

Chapter 2: In the Romanian Army 13

Chapter 3: The Russians Come 31

Chapter 4: Drafted Again 41

Chapter 5: On the Western Front 57

Chapter 6: Flight of the Women and Children 67

Chapter 7: Prying the Family Loose
           From the Communists 81

Chapter 8: Refugee Life 89

Chapter 9: Land of Opportunity 103

Chapter 10: Surviving as a Farmer Today 115

Chapter 11: The Next Generation 123

Chapter 12: German Success Breeds Hatred 133

Chapter 13: Visiting the Communists 137

Chapter 14: Bad Dreams 143

Bibliography 147

This book is better than most. Wieland's notes appear to be objective, scholarly, & pretty well balanced.

Weiss seems to be a special person. He does OK.

Book is pretty much pro-German.

9H Popphe

Introduction

I still dream that the Russians are after me, like when the Germans drafted me and I was on the Eastern Front in February of 1944. Our unit was outnumbered maybe five to one. The Russian tanks broke through at 6 a.m. on the second day of the fighting. They were only one hundred meters away; in the next seconds they would overrun us.

Our officer commanded, "Don't shoot. Our tanks shoot first." We were about sixty men — not a full company, dug in for about a thousand yards to either side of the road. Our tanks fired and exploded the first three Russian tanks, and the Russian troops behind spread out in the snow. They had on dark uniforms, so we could still see them. There was a dip, and they kept coming over the top towards us. We fought for three or four hours — we had plenty of ammunition. They finally stopped coming.

The lieutenant had our sergeant report. Because the sergeant was a Lithuanian, he didn't understand German well. He came back and said we were supposed to hold the position a couple of hours more.

"Impossible."

"Why don't you go over and ask, yourself?"

Just as I started, I met the *Melder* (messenger).

"Get out! Get out! They all left already."

So we all started to run out of our foxholes. Right then the first Russian hand grenades came. The guy next to me was hit. His leg was blown off. We dragged him back in a snow-boat as quickly as we could go. Five men stayed back and fired to save the rest of us. They were supposed to follow, but I never saw them again.

Immanuel Weiss suffers from other nightmares — of being an unarmed Romanian soldier facing a Russian tank when his Bessarabian homeland was invaded, of being left to defend a

i

bridge over the Rhine while the rest of the German army retreated behind him, of rescuing his wife and children from communist-occupied East Germany.

This book will use the words of Immanuel Weiss and his wife Johanna to describe the life of the Bessarabian peasants as they went from the peaceful years of the 1930s to the Soviet invasion of 1940, of being "saved" and resettled by the Nazis in Poland, and then of living through the madness of the fighting on Germany's East Front. Luck played an important role in determining who survived the bloodbath of World War II, but Immanuel and Johanna's peasant values helped: when it comes to war, don't volunteer.

Their peasant values also help us understand how, after losing their farm in Bessarabia, they could begin anew in Poland, and, after losing that farm, continue to struggle and survive as penniless refugees in West Germany. Their peasant values especially explain why they chose to become Americans and why they attempted once more to become independent farmers in America. The background of these peasant values is covered in the first chapter of the Weisses' story.

A note on method: The words of this story come from five years of interviews, letters, phone conversations, and written memories. My main contribution has been to provide the broader historical and sociological background in a series of chapter introductions. I have kept a few of the original German words in the text to preserve a little of the original tone for the reader.

Chapter 1

Bessarabia

Immanuel and Johanna's ancestors left Swabia in southwestern Germany at the beginning of the nineteenth century to take up the Russian Tsar's offer of free land in Bessarabia. Five generations later, Immanuel and Johanna and their fellow Bessarabian Germans still typified the Swabian culture and values: they were independent-minded, religious, fanatic about work, and frugal.

The Swabians of Württemberg, Germany, along with the neighboring Alsatians and Swiss, are all Alemannic Germans, with a very independent-minded culture. The Alemanni followed the custom of dividing property equally among the children at death. Consequently, a society of independent peasants developed. In much of the remainder of Germany, one son inherited the farm and the others worked for him or left to work in the cities. A different culture resulted there, one in which people learned to give and take orders. In keeping with the relative independence of the Swabian peasants, the Swabian nobility extracted taxes but did not press the peasants harshly or expect them to perform menial or personal services, as in some other parts of Germany.

The Swabian peasants' relative independence also encouraged hard work and the husbanding of resources, since these actions benefited the peasant directly. In addition, the practice of equal inheritance tended to reduce the average size of the peasant holdings over the generations, so the peasants were forced to work harder and more efficiently, and be more frugal, just to survive.

The Protestant Reformation reinforced these values in Swabia. People spoke to God directly, and they were responsible directly to God for their actions. Their guide was the "inner light," the religious spirit within, rather than the expectations of formal religious organizations. Just as each peasant was responsible for his own land, so was he directly responsible for his ethical and religious behavior.

But the political and social changes of the Napoleonic era—the reduction of the role of religion in everyday life—threatened the piety of the Swabians. Because the state-run Lutheran Church rejected the Separatists and their undisciplined religious fervor, many emigrated from their country of Württemberg to other lands which promised religious freedom. Many went east to the Black Sea area of Russia, to Bessarabia or the Ukraine, or farther, to the Caucasus. They wanted to live a purer life and await the imminent Second Coming of Christ. Other Swabians with similar beliefs immigrated to establish the religious communes of Harmony and Zoar on the American frontier.

The Protestant Ethic was so strong in Swabian society that it affected all Swabians, even less-religious ones and members of religious minorities. Albert Einstein, born of Jewish parents, claimed his success was due simply to hard work; and Bertolt Brecht, born of a Catholic father, bragged that he did some writing every day, even during the many years he was homeless and fleeing the Nazis from country to country. Both these men also exemplified the typical Swabian disdain for the material life. They preferred simple, frugal living. As a Swabian motto has it, "Sell the dog, and bark yourself." These values, cherished by Swabians and so many other immigrants to America, appear over and over in the story told by Immanuel and Johanna.

Origins

In 1815 our ancestors settled near the Black Sea. My great-great-great-grandparents, on both my father's and my mother's side, left Württemberg when Tsar Alexander invited the Germans to colonize Bessarabia. We still spoke *Schwäbisch* (Swabian), even though I was the fifth generation to live in Bessarabia.

A few Bessarabian Germans spoke *Plattdeutsch* or *Kaschuban* because their ancestors came from north Germany, but over time, most of the people came to speak *Schwäbisch*—like Johanna's father who grew up speaking *Platt*, but started to speak *Schwäbisch* after he married Johanna's mother.

Our forefathers left Germany because of their religion, and religion kept them together in Bessarabia. In Germany, the

2

church was supported by the government. But in Bessarabia, the church was private, supported by the people directly. For many years under the Russians, the schools were private — run by our church — and that helped to keep the people together. But the Russian government took them over in the last part of the nineteenth century.

I was born in 1916, while Bessarabia was still part of Russia, just before Bessarabia became independent and joined Romania. My father was a harness maker, and his father before him, too, but they also farmed. Everybody was a farmer.

I went to school for eight years, until I was fifteen. Up to 1925 we had only German teachers. Then we had less and less German and more and more instruction in Romanian; they were trying to make us Romanians. Bessarabia was originally Romanian, way back in the 1400s. It was called Moldavia. Then it belonged to the Turks until the Russians conquered it in 1812. And then Romania took it back at the end of the First World War, in 1918, and the Romanians wanted to make sure we stayed Romanian.

Johanna and Erna pose in the yard of the Weiss house in Kulm, Bessarabia, September 1940.

Farm Life

We lived on the steppe; it was prairie with no trees except what we planted in the ravines. We had about three hundred families in our village, and the average farm was about 80 acres. That's what Johanna and I had, and we also rented another 40 acres from my brother. We grew barley — which we mostly sold—winter wheat, corn, soybeans, and oats for the horses. Everybody shared rights to the village common land—the pastures. There was one for everyone's sheep and another for the horses and cows. We owned three cows for milk, and twenty or so sheep for the wool—for sweaters, socks, mittens, and so on. The women in every family would spin the wool and use it for knitting. Some even did weaving. We also raised pigs for our meat, plus some as a cash crop—maybe a half dozen or more. We had chickens and sold eggs, and sold some of our wine, too. And, of course, we raised all our vegetables and fruit ourselves.

Horses were very important to us in Bessarabia. All the children—including the girls—learned to ride horses. When the corn was cultivated, a kid maybe seven to ten years old would ride the horse and lead it through the corn rows—same thing for cultivating in the vineyards. When we harvested the wheat, a kid would ride the first of the four horses so the man on the mower could pay full attention to his machine.

We were glad to ride the horses in the beginning. But when it was day after day after day, then it was work! The heat was bad—it was as hot as a hundred degrees in the summer in Bessarabia. The horseflies and the wild bees would bite you, and the sweat from the horses would sting your legs and your body.

A seasoned Bessarabian team powers a three-bottom plow during spring planting.

We put animal manure to good use in Bessarabia—we used it for fuel. Our village was on the steppe, and there were few trees for firewood, so we made *Brennmist* (manure for burning). We piled up the manure all winter, and it rotted and got all soft, just like butter. Then we laid straw down—so the *Brennmist* wouldn't stick to the ground later. Next we raked out a layer of manure twelve inches thick on top of the straw. The horses pulled a three-foot round stone to roll the manure from time to time. In two or three weeks, it was packed down hard and solid, four inches thick. We'd use a hatchet to slice it into blocks, which we lifted up to dry all summer. It was real nice stuff with no smell, and it burned well.

Brennmist was what we burned in the winter. It was the only thing that would burn all day long. Our trees weren't much good for firewood—acacia, mulberry, and so on. We used them just for a quick cooking fire. We also used cornstalks after the cattle had eaten the leaves off.

We burned our *Brennmist* in a *Kachelofen* (a big stove of tiled bricks) built into the walls somewhere in the middle of the house so at least two, maybe three or four, rooms could be heated. Ceramic tiles covered the bricks to look nice and make it easy to clean. The *Brennmist* would heat the bricks and tiles, and you'd get a good, steady heat into your rooms.

Johanna describes some of the foods of the Bessarabian Germans—and the work of the women:

In our Bessarabian food, we like the smell and taste of garlic. One of our specialities is *Dampfknödele* (steam dumplings) on top of sauerkraut. They're made from flour and warm water and a little salt. When the sauerkraut and ribs are nearly done, you put the dough on top, and for twenty minutes you keep the lid on. You don't open it till they're done.

Strudel is another specialty. You add oil to the dough so it stretches better. You start with dough the size of a tennis ball. You stretch it as big as a table, so thin you can see through. You cut half off and put it on top of the other half and roll it more. You cut strips about four or five inches wide, put them on top of your potatoes and meat, and cover the pot.

We also make *Knöpfle* (Swabian noodles or dumplings). You roll out two feet of dough and you cut it in strips two inches wide and then cut pieces off one-eighth-inch at a time. They're like little noodles, and we cook them in salt water. Then we roast some butter and bread crumbs in the frying pan and pour it over the drained *Knöpfle*. We have a lot of foods with dough, more than we do with potatoes.

Here in America we sometimes have *Knöpfle* with potatoes. First we'll cook the potatoes, then use the same water to cook the *Knöpfle*. Then we'll mix them up, fry some onions, and pour the hot onions over the potatoes and *Knöpfle*. We eat it together with sauerkraut.

We eat *Fastnachts* (donuts) a lot, not just at *Fastnacht* (Carnival or Mardi Gras). They taste good any time. We'll have them with a soup meal; we eat them like bread.

Self-Reliance

In Bessarabia, we made use of everything. To make our featherbeds, we would go *Federschlitzen* (goose-feather collecting) every eight weeks or so. We took feathers from underneath the geese, and also half of the feathers from the front, and also on top, between the wings. But you had to be careful there. If you took too much, the wings fell down. Afterwards the geese didn't look so good for a while, but the feathers always grew back.

The featherbeds were part of what we called *Aussteuer* (dowry), which we made ourselves when we were young—all our towels, blankets, and bedding. We even wove our own dresses.

Flax was important for these things. We would pick it in late summer and then dry it in five- or six-inch thick bundles. Then we laid the flax in a pond, covered with mud for three weeks. After washing and drying, the fibers on the stem would come loose. Three different hand tools were used to prepare the fibers. Then we could spin them on the wheel. We would weave them in different widths to make sacks and single-bed or double-bed sheets. We'd spread the big thirty-foot lengths of cloth outside and dampen them with water every so often, so that the sun could bleach them into nice white sheets.

We also had homemade cornhusk mattresses. We used the soft white corn leaves, cut them in half-inch wide strips and put them in a sack. We used cornhusk leaves instead of straw because sleeping on straw would soon turn it into chaff, into dust. The cornhusk leaves could last up to a year. We'd have enough husks saved so we could exchange new for old during the year. For sure, every harvest time we had brand-new mattresses. The mattresses were like almost everything else we used — from nature and healthy and produced by our own hands.

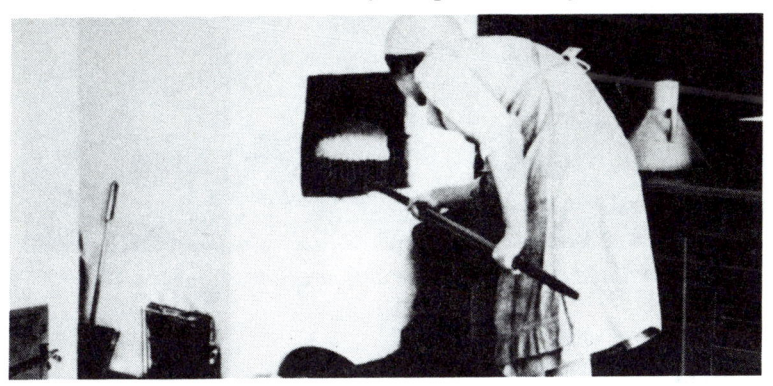

In Bessarabia, bread was baked usually once a week from homegrown wheat ground in each village. Each family had its own brick oven in the house or the summer kitchen.

Immanuel describes village and family life:

We didn't have a *Wirtschaft* (restaurant and saloon) in the village. Everybody produced their own food and drink. The farmers' wives baked their own bread and also their own cakes. They cooked all the meals, too. Everybody took their meals as a family at home.

People also produced their own wine, lots of it. In the winter, men and their wives, and also young people over fifteen or so, would meet at some neighbors'. The men would talk politics and drink wine. The women knitted sweaters, gloves, or socks while they talked.

Wine was our drink. We would mix wine and water half-and-half and have a glass or two at meal time. Even the kids used to get a swallow now and then. Most families had their own wine press, because almost everybody stored from five hundred to five thousand or more liters every year.

The Kulm village church was the center of life.

Strictness

We had no playing cards, none in the house. They were the Devil's work and not allowed in a religious family. Actually, I never even saw cards until I was nineteen and visited in Germany in 1935. And I was twenty-four before I ever played cards — when we were stuck in the refugee camp in Germany.

My mother was very religious, and from the evening of *Gründonnerstag* (Maundy Thursday) to the evening of Good Friday, she wouldn't eat a thing. We children got fed — but, of course, no meat on Good Friday. Also, on Good Friday, on Easter Day, and on Christmas Day, we weren't allowed to play ball, or even touch a toy. On those days we had to go twice to church, in the morning and also in the afternoon.

We were strictly punished when we were guilty of doing something bad or of not doing what we were told. We had to go to the corner of the room and kneel on corn kernels. That hurt!

Our father's punishment was even worse — with a strap. There's a saying, "If you love your child, you take care of it." And another saying: " The harder the rod, the better the child."

8

As a child I didn't believe that. But because our parents were so strict then, we got to know at a young age what was right and what was wrong, what was allowed and what was not. The teachers in the school had the same pointed proverb: "If you can't hear, you must feel." Then came the rod!

Another thing: Sunday was special to us. We planned the whole week around not working on Sunday. On Saturday, we spent most of the day doing special jobs. The youngest child polished all the shoes — we carried that over here to America, too. We swept up the whole *Hof* (the farmyard) and spread nice yellow sand. In the house on Sundays, we could take our shoes off and walk on floor mats made of corn husks. Everything was nice on Sundays.

While we didn't have cards in Bessarabia, we did have dancing. During the winter, teenagers rented a hall for Sunday afternoons and evenings. In the summer there was a danceplace out on the *Wiese* (the meadow) near some trees. We had accordions and harmonicas for music. There was also a brass band with twenty-one instruments, and I used to play the horn.

Then we had radio programs from Germany, from Leipzig, Halle, and so on. My oldest brother had the first radio in the village. The German radio music was different from ours. They played marches, while we had polkas and waltzes.

I remember the neighbor said, "My gosh, they all talk German. How can it be?" See, we were like an island. Everybody around was non-German, and this radio broadcast came from the outside, too. Well, when we heard German on the radio, we felt stronger. It was a fight for survival in Bessarabia for the Germans. The Romanians ordered, "No German language allowed." The head of our Evangelical (Lutheran) Church and also our political leaders were always going to the capital, Bucharest, to fight for the German language.

Different Nationalities

If you went through a village you could tell if it was German — or Bulgarian, or Turkish. In German villages, the buildings all had whitewash, the other villages had gray or brownish-red buildings. Some villages — the Bulgarian ones — were good, but some — the Turkish ones — were not kept up. They had a sloppy style.

Some Bulgarians and Russians worked for Germans, and they were good, hard workers. We had to hoe the corn two times by hand — thirty acres of corn — so we hired help. They walked on the streets in the morning — teenagers and married women. We'd call them over, "How much do you want today?" When we agreed, we all had breakfast at the house, and then we'd take a big barrel of water and our lunch and work all day, from sun-up to sun-down. They also slept in our buildings, and the next morning they'd work again if they were needed; otherwise they'd go on.

They got about 30 *lei* per day. To give you an idea, a pair of shoes cost 300 *lei*, so you had to work half a month for them. Of course, besides their pay they got food, and they were fed pretty well. The hired help ate at the same table with us. There were no class-differences. Well, there were some very rich people where maybe there was a difference. But not in our village.

We didn't speak German with these people. The Romanian language was used between different peoples. The Bulgarians knew Romanian, and the Germans, too. But I also knew a few words of Bulgarian and pretty good Russian. I knew enough for on the farm. I learned the words from the hired help. There were also Turks living nearby, but they didn't work with us. A Jewish butcher lived in our village, too, and two or three other Jews used to come to the village to buy grain or hides.

In 1931, a couple of months before his fifteenth birthday, Immanuel was confirmed in the church, finished his schooling, and became an adult. He wanted to apprentice and learn a craft, like cabinetmaker or locksmith, but his father wasn't well enough to do all the farm work alone and Immanuel was the only child left at home.

Three years later, he was able to get away for a year as an apprentice on a training farm near Lüneburg in Germany. There, he found "one could speak German without worrying about it." *He was also surprised when he reported to the head office of the organization in Hamburg and was given 2000* **Reichsmarks**

($500) to deliver to the farm's manager. That was impressive. What trust the Germans had!

There he learned modern farming techniques unknown in Bessarabia, and he met boys and girls from all over the German-speaking world, including Latvia and Switzerland, as well as Transylvania and the Banat in Romania. He also learned about North German customs such as eating Lüneburger cheese for breakfast ("I almost couldn't eat it, and if I'd been alone, I'd have thrown it away.")

He was able to make bike trips around North Germany. But when a group of trainees biked to Denmark, he was turned back at the border because of his Romanian citizenship. He also became more politically aware. He got to see Hitler at a peasant festival and learned more about him over the course of the year.

Foreboding

Hitler was a good speaker. I saw how the Germans believed everything he said. He had promised them jobs and food, and that's what they had; they were building highways and canals and other things. Germany was a happy nation in 1935.

I heard Hitler's speech on the first of April. All the factories stopped to hear his speech; it was about 11 a.m.

"Starting today," he said, "we are going to have an army, and nobody is going to stop us." He told the young men to come and join, and I remember how they were screaming and happy. There was a twenty-five-year-old foreman near us: "I'm gonna volunteer right away."

Everybody was drafted anyway for half a year in the *Arbeitsdienst* (state labor service). Women went to do housework for farm families; men did farm work or manual labor. There was almost no more unemployment, and pretty soon everybody was happy. A worker was earning four or five *Reichsmarks* (RM) per day. He could buy a pair of pants for that. A car cost only RM1000, and could be bought for RM250 down — for fifty days of pay. But in the factories they also built weapons — tanks and things. And if you build them, you have to use them.

11

Chapter 2

In The Romanian Army

Immanuel returned to his Bessarabian homeland to work on his father's farm. The next year's harvest was bad, and Immanuel often thought that he should have stayed in Germany where he could have found a good job. But he had been homesick in Germany.

From the age of eighteen, Immanuel, like other young men, had to take part in quasi-military exercises under Romanian command. Even though he was of German ancestry, Immanuel was expected to serve in the Romanian military, for Bessarabia, and the Romanian nation to which it belonged, were multicultural, like the United States.

Modern-day Romania arose in 1859, from the uniting of the principalities of Walachia and Moldavia. These two states go far back in the Middle Ages, and the people trace their origins and language to the time of the Roman Empire. Both Walachia and Moldavia came under the control of the Turks for several centuries, but in the eighteenth and nineteenth centuries, the Ottoman Empire gradually loosened its grip on southeastern Europe. In 1812, Russia freed a part of Moldavia — Bessarabia — and incorporated it into its own growing empire. To improve agriculture, the Tsar invited German and Bulgarian peasants, granting them land, freedom from military service, freedom of worship, and no taxes for ten years. As a result of this history, Bessarabia came to have a very mixed population. At the time Immanuel was growing up (1930s), the Bessarabian population was 56 percent Romanian, 24 percent Ukrainian or Russian, 7 percent Jewish, 6 percent Bulgarian, 4 percent Gagausian (Turkish Christians), and 3 percent German.

Subsequent Russian victories eliminated Turkish control of the rest of Moldavia and of Walachia. Instead of being absorbed by the Russian Empire, as Bessarabia had been, Moldavia and

Walachia joined together into a kingdom, the beginning of the modern state of Romania.

World War I provided Romania the opportunity to bring the remainder of the Romanian people into their own nation. Defeated Austro-Hungary yielded Transylvania. Because Russia was also a defeated nation, parts of the Russian Empire were able to declare their independence — in the north, Finland and the Baltic lands of Estonia, Latvia, and Lithuania; and in the south, Bessarabia, first seeking independence, and then annexation by Romania.

The majority Romanians in Bessarabia were especially happy to be joined with their compatriots, but many of the other people were happy to escape the oppression and discrimination of the Russians. There had been, for example, a major anti-Jewish pogrom in 1903. Germans had found the rights guaranteed them, in 1813 by Tsar Alexander I, being withdrawn as time passed. All of the peasants feared exploitation and being reduced to the feudal status of the Russian peasants.

For these reasons, most Bessarabians had supported the liberal Kerensky government that came to power during the first Russian Revolution of March, 1917. A Bessarabian government was set up, which demanded more autonomy, land reform, and use of the Romanian language. But when the second, more extremist revolution — the November Bolshevik Revolution — developed, the Bessarabians declared their independence from the new Soviet Union and, in 1918, turned to Romania.

Romania, fearing the spread of the Soviet Revolution and communist ideology, instituted a major land reform and broke up farms over 250 acres in size, thus benefiting many landless or poor peasants in Bessarabia. Minorities, like the German Bessarabians, also were given the opportunity to vote. Romania was more or less a democracy, and from 1923 on, all men could vote. Unfortunately, there was a long tradition of political corruption in Romania, and by the 1930s it would become apparent to the Bessarabians that their province was essentially a backward colony exploited by politicians from Moldavia and Walachia.

Romania's sovereignty over Bessarabia was recognized internationally in the Paris Treaty of 1920, signed by Great Britain, France, Italy, and Japan — but not the Soviet Union. The Soviets never really reconciled themselves to the loss of Bessarabia. They *even instigated a short-lived communist revolt in the Bessarabian town of Tatar-Bunar in 1924.*

Romania prudently joined several alliances to forestall aggression from its neighbors. Romania and Poland signed a mutual defense treaty since they were both menaced by the Soviet Union. Romania, also, signed defense treaties with Yugoslavia and Czechoslovakia for protection against Hungary and Bulgaria — which coveted those parts of Romania containing Hungarian and Bulgarian minorities, respectively.

Thus Romania wanted to help when its ally Czechoslovakia was threatened by Hitler in 1938. The Romanians even secretly agreed to let Soviet troops cross their territory to stop Hitler. After Britain's Chamberlain met Hitler and agreed to "peace for our time" at Munich, Czechoslovakia was dismembered by Germany, Poland, and Hungary. But Romania refused to take the piece of Czechoslovakian territory offered by Poland.

However, Romania's options were narrowing. Over the course of the 1930s, she had become increasingly economically dependent on Germany to sell her wheat and oil. The events of 1938 showed that there could be no counterbalancing power on the European continent: Romania had to accept German influence. When Poland was invaded and divided by Hitler and Stalin in September of 1939, Romania was powerless to aid her ally and had to declare neutrality. Romania was helpless before the actions of the power mongers of Europe, Hitler and Stalin.

By 1940, Romania could see that its immediate danger lay close at hand — the Soviet Union, which was expanding westward. After annexing eastern Poland, the Soviet Union had invaded Finland. Even expulsion from the League of Nations didn't stop the Soviets. They also demanded military bases and communist front governments in the Baltic nations of Estonia, Latvia, and Lithuania, as a prelude to annexation. All these territories had been lost at the end of the First World War, when Russia was becoming the Soviet Union. The Soviets were only taking back what the tsars had ruled.

In 1934, when I was eighteen, I had to do pre-military training for the Romanian army — every Sunday from 8 a.m. until noon. It wasn't bad, but I had to walk a couple of miles to the next German town to do it. That was because our lieutenant, a Romanian, taught school and lived there. As Germans, we were not to be trusted. We had to train under a Romanian officer. Because of the training, I missed church, too.

We had good training. We even practiced with make-believe guns we carved out of wood, and in our summer camp, we were decorated as the best unit. Our lieutenant got promoted because of us.

The Cavalry

When I was twenty, we were mustered for inspection by a commission of officers and doctors. My assignment was the cavalry, and I was ordered to supply a horse, too. The Romanians called it *"Calarasch ku skimb,"* or "the rider changes." That meant my horse was used both by me and a second soldier.

Immanuel Weiss on his cavalry horse (at right) with other riders of the Romanian "Calarasch Ku Skimb" *from Kulm. 1938.*

It was an expensive assignment for me: I had to keep that horse in A-1 condition, always ready for call up. I had to have my own tailored uniform made, as well as riding boots and headgear. I had to supply most of my own food—and the feed for the horse, too. The state really profited from us Germans that way. Of the sixty-four in our squadron, forty were Germans and the rest were Bulgarians, Romanians, and Russians who used our horses to train.

There was a big advantage to *"Calarasch ku skimb"* for us. We were allowed to serve just six months active duty instead of eighteen months, and the rest of the time we would be in the reserves and farming our land. Of course, in a general alert or call-up, the part-time active duty would end. We learned that later on.

So in April of 1938, I was drafted into the regular army like all other able-bodied men. It wasn't pleasant at all. The Romanians were very corrupt. Bribes were forbidden by the government, but expected by everyone. The noncoms would refuse to let us or our horses pass inspection, and we might have to pay 100 or 200 *lei*. That was a lot of money then—a worker earned only 700 or 800 *lei* in a month.

In April of 1938, Immanuel (front row, third from right) was drafted into the regular Romanian Army. His platoon included twelve Bessarabian Germans.

And the sergeants were always finding little ways to force us to give them money. For example, our riding boots had yellow stars in the front below the knee. Before we'd stand watch, we would grab a few hours sleep without changing our clothes. But when we got up, the stars on our boots were gone—or maybe the ones from the shoulders. They had taken them off. For

17

Appell (roll call) at 7 a.m., everything had to be in order. So we were reported to the sergeant, and it cost 10 or 20 *lei* to get our stuff back! The Romanians were really corrupt.

Our usual day would begin at 4 a.m., when we got up. For breakfast—about 4:30 a.m.—we had a half cup of sweet tea and a slice of plain bread. Nothing on it, just a piece of plain bread. That's all until midday, when we had *Tschorba* or *ciorba* (a vegetable or bean soup) and some bread. That was three times a week. Part of the week, we had *mamaliga* (a corn mush) instead for lunch. The evening meal wasn't any better—it was usually just as little as lunch was. We always had to buy extra food to survive. After three months of training camp, I weighed scarcely 100 or 110 pounds. I lost about 40 pounds there.

After two months of good behavior, they allowed us to leave the camp and live in private rooms. We had rented one, from the beginning, to store the food we bought privately—and to store the horse feed, too. Otherwise, the horse and I wouldn't have made it.

They treated us Germans badly. They took us for fascists and followers of Hitler, even though we had nothing to do with that business. But we Germans learned fast, and of all the nationalities, we performed the best. The only exceptions were some Romanians or Bulgarians who were about equal to us.

After three months of basic training, we went home to harvest grain for two months. At that point my father's health was very bad and then he died on the sixth of August. I had been engaged to Johanna for two years, and we decided, since my stepmother and a hired hand were alone on the farm, to push the wedding ahead. We married on the fourteenth of August, 1938.

We were together only two weeks. I had to be back for maneuvers starting September first, at Ismail on the Danube some sixty miles away. Later I got a letter from her, saying how she and the dog stood at the gate to the farm, crying together from loneliness. Her parents had been dead since 1933—and my father and mother were gone, too. It was not a nice time for either of us.

Then I had an accident. Three of our cavalry squadrons at Ismail were to have a mock battle with three squadrons from Galatz (Galati). Every day we had extra practice, including jumping over the bush-barriers and ditches. There was a triple barricade. The first pole was a meter high, the next pole a meter and a quarter high, then a pole a meter and a half high. We did this lots of time before. But somehow—whether it was my fault, the horse's, or both of us, I don't know—but we had an accident. The last pole got caught between my horse's front legs, and I flew in the air maybe thirty feet. I didn't wake up till I was in the hospital in Ismail. Thanks to God, nothing was broken, just plenty of bruises for both me and my horse.

The fall maneuvers lasted until the fifteenth of October, when we could go home. Of course, we always had to be in a state of readiness. But we would still be at home to put in the crops next spring, too.

The tenth of May was a big national holiday, *"Zara Romania Mare,"* celebrating the unification of the ten Romanian provinces united into Greater Romania after the First World War. So we had to go back in again for five to ten days. We drilled and prepared our equipment—our curved, three-foot-long swords, our rifles, saddles, and all—for the parade. Afterwards, we handed our equipment back and we could go home.

War Comes to Europe

That fall in 1939, we were supposed to go on our yearly maneuvers again, but Germany invaded Poland. So the Romanian Army was put on full alert. We didn't know whether the Poles would try to come into our country. They were being squeezed from both sides; the Russians were also attacking Poland from the east. *(The Polish government did in fact take refuge in Romania.)*

Many of our troops were also sent to the Dniester River, our border with Russia. Our cavalry assignment was unit headquarters at Ismail on the Danube, a hundred miles to the south of the border with Russia.

While we were stationed there, our general bought some hay for the horses from one of our German villages.

"You guys are from that area," he told us, "and I don't want to pay someone to haul the hay."

So we volunteered, twenty-four soldiers together, two for each wagon. Normally the trip of sixty miles out and sixty back would take four days. But we told our noncom, "We need ten days, because we need time at home, too. We're farmers and our wives are home running the farms."

"No, you can't."

"What if we bring back ten pounds of butter?"

"Okay."

We didn't load the wagons very full. That way, we could make a lot of trips. We made six or eight of them before the hay all got to Ismail. And the noncom got geese, chickens, ham—all kinds of food besides butter. See, you had to *schmier* (bribe), if you wanted anything.

So we were kept on full alert for the rest of 1939. The arrangement that we only serve full-time for a month and a half out of the year was naturally cancelled. Most of the men in our unit were kept on the Dniester, digging defenses. The government started calling up older and older guys, even guys as old as thirty-six. The whole of Romania was mobilized. Because we had to stay on active duty, Johanna and hired help had to put in the crops the next year, in 1940.

When we got up on the morning of the twenty-eighth of June, 1940, we heard all kinds of noise—automobiles and wagons travelling about. Normally it would be quiet in Ismail. Our landlady, a Romanian officer's wife, told us, "The Russians crossed the border. Our army has four days to clear out of Bessarabia."

We didn't know it, but there was a secret agreement signed between Hitler and Stalin. Our country had no choice.

Almost a year earlier, on August 23, 1939, Germany and the Soviet Union signed a non-aggression and mutual assistance pact. A secret supplement was also signed late in September, allotting the different countries in Eastern Europe to Soviet or German spheres of influence. Hitler and Stalin could then do whatever they wanted to the peoples within these new territories.

Paragraph Three of the supplement stated:

With regard to South Eastern Europe, the Soviets on their part emphasize their interest in Bessarabia. The Germans on their part declare themselves completely disinterested in these territories.

Stalin did not move on Bessarabia immediately. First came Poland. In a very deft maneuver, Stalin waited almost three weeks after the German invasion of Poland on September 1, 1939, stalling despite repeated pleas by Hitler to take up the assigned eastern part of Poland so as not to give the Polish army any respite. Stalin didn't want Polish allies such as Britain to see his invasion as aggression, but as helping the Poles. Because the Germans advanced so far and so quickly into Poland, and even into the eastern territories assigned to the Soviet Union, Stalin could wait no more. On September 17, 1939, the Red Army moved into eastern Poland, and the deportations of enemies of the state began—including nationalistic Ukrainians as well as Poles. On November 3, 1939, the territory was annexed to the Soviet Union, and in the ensuing year, about 1.5 million Poles were deported to Russia. This was, incidentally, roughly equal to the number of Jews and Poles that Hitler was deporting from German-annexed western Poland to be replaced with ethnic Germans from the new Soviet conquests.

On November 30, Stalin launched his winter war against Finland. The Finns finally admitted defeat on March 11, 1940. In just two weeks, the Finns had to evacuate over 0.5 million people from the lost territories. Stalin would replace them with Russians.

Ever since the signing of the Soviet-German nonaggression pact and the assignment of spheres of influence, Stalin had been escalating his pressures against the neighboring Baltic states of Estonia, Latvia, and Lithuania. The Red Army finally occupied them in mid-June, 1940. Stalin set in motion plans to have one third of the populations of these countries sent to Siberia, to be replaced by Russians. The new borders and population shifts agreed on by Hitler and Stalin were almost complete; only the Bessarabian part of the agreement with Hitler remained to be fulfilled.

Stalin now had a special incentive to move fast on Bessarabia — Hitler had so quickly conquered Denmark, Norway, the Netherlands, Belgium, and France in the West, that he might change his mind about allotting so much territory to the Soviet Union in the East. Hitler's gains in the West would soon be digested.

On the evening of June 26, 1940, the Soviet Union gave Romania a twenty-four hour ultimatum to vacate Bessarabia, and as the Soviets expected, the German government spent the next day actively urging the Romanians not to fight. The Germans especially worried that resistance would lead the Soviets to push beyond Bessarabia, and fighting might damage the vital Ploesti oil fields. The Romanian government finally agreed to vacate Bessarabia, to allow the Soviets to move their border south to the Prut and Danube Rivers.

We were twelve friends in the cavalry, all Germans, and we didn't want to go with our unit across the Danube to Romania. We wanted to stay with our own people. But if we deserted the Romanian Army, we would be helping the Soviet Union. We didn't want to do that either.

So we went down to the squadron. There was a whole mess of saddles, horseshoes, clothes, boots, and so on, and we helped take them all down to the boat, ready for evacuation across the Danube. The road was old and rough and there was all kinds of confusion when the axle broke on a wagon full of horseshoes. But we got them down to the river.

Rather than go with the horseshoes across the Danube, we Germans decided we'd better stay and load hay. It got late in the day and we had to decide one way or another soon, before the Romanian Army left Bessarabia. We decided to desert — that same night. We had to be with our families when the Russians came.

One of my best friends, Dompert, was a clerk. I told him of our plans. He wanted to come along: "Would you wait for me? I'll try to get away as soon as I can." Another friend, Sawall, lived two houses down. We three decided to go together.

I was too scared to sleep in my room. I thought maybe our noncoms would come at night and take me across the Danube, over the new border into Romania. So I went out to the

22

landlady's big garden and lay down under the bushes. I was scared because maybe I wouldn't be able to go home again. I waited for Dompert to come, but then I drifted off to sleep.

Then I could hear Dompert yelling my name; I didn't know if I was dreaming or what. After a while, I finally realized it really happened. So I ran to Sawall's place. He and Dompert were still there!

Well, we were worried. It was already getting towards daybreak; the nights were short in June. We took the quickest way out of the city, heading eastward, towards home. The three of us walked through Ismail, one behind the other.

After a few blocks we saw a Romanian patrol coming towards us along the other side of the street. At night, patrols went out to catch deserters. So we stayed on our side of the street and just kept going towards them. They were three men, and we were three men. Like them, we also had officer's caps, nice tailor-made uniforms, and high boots. So they didn't stop us. We marched by each other! It was still dark enough that they thought we were a patrol from another unit.

It was daylight when we got to the edge of the city; we had to disappear. So we crawled into a field of grain and lay down. It was hot and we were thirsty; and hungry, too, because we hadn't gotten any food the day before. Finally, the three of us couldn't stand it any more, and about four in the afternoon, we got up and started walking away from the city. We went down into a valley where there were some trees and bushes.

Heading Home

After we walked some way east towards home, we saw a wagon and some people in a cornfield. We came up to them, and they cried out, "Don't take our horses." When they saw our uniforms, they thought the worst would happen.

"We just want something to drink."

"Have all you want," they told us. So we did and then we walked on some six miles farther.

For the twenty-some miles in this stretch, there were only two places to get food and drink, two *Wirtschafts* (inns). When we reached the first, I went in, because I knew the owner. When he saw me in my uniform, he quickly told me, "Disappear, disappear. A patrol just got some soldiers. Tied them hand and foot and took them off to Ismail." Quickly I grabbed a bottle of wine and left.

We went into the brush and hid until it was dark. Then we started along the road again, but staying in the fields, not on the road. That way, we would keep going in the right direction. And we could see what was on the main street without being seen ourselves. We saw Romanian troops heading towards Ismail, but they didn't see us.

But we had to go onto the road whenever we came to a stream; we had to use the bridges. About midnight we got close to the second *Wirtschaft*, located on a stream. Then in the distance we heard a rumbling—heavy wood and steel wheels rolling on the road. Something was coming. Russians or Romanians? We wouldn't care to meet either.

We decided to head for a nearby village where a Bulgarian comrade from our squadron lived. He deserted before we did and was probably home already. So we crossed over the road and started toward the village. The rumbling kept coming closer and closer. We went parallel to the stream, heading upstream from the bridge. The water would be shallower there. It was a *liman* (where the water from the Black Sea backs up into a creek).

We went maybe a hundred yards. We just had finished taking off our clothes to cross when we spotted a soldier—in a Romanian artillery uniform—pretty close to us.

"What are you doing here?" he asked.

"We want to get across to the village."

"Well, you'd better hurry. And don't worry, it's not too deep. That's my village over there. I have to go now, my comrades are calling me. If I don't get back, we'll all be in trouble."

Before he left, we asked, "How did you spot us?"

"The moon was shining on the water behind you!"

So we quickly went farther back into the fields, farther away from the road. Again we took off our clothes and started walking across. It was only a small moon shining, but still strong enough to cast our shadows in the water. We walked over anyway, as the moon got higher.

On the other side, we walked and walked. We got confused. But finally we reached the Bulgarian village. We stopped at a peasant's house. The dogs saw us and barked, and then the owner came out. We asked, "Are there any police still in the village?"

"No, they cleared out." So we felt free to go and visit our friend, Malumin Dimitri.

He was happy to see us. We told him we'd like to eat and then rest — we really needed to sleep after walking all night.

"No, first we have to go to the *liman* — to swim and enjoy ourselves. After all, we're free now!"

We didn't really want to — we were still twenty-five miles from home. But we went along anyway. It was Sunday, and a whole bunch of guys were there from the village. A lot of them had red bands around their arms or chests, to show they were communist sympathizers. Plenty of Bulgarians were sympathizers, so even if these guys weren't communists, they would wear the red bands to be safe. Either way, we weren't too happy.

Besides, we still had our Romanian cavalry uniforms on; so they knew we were deserters. We didn't feel proud to be deserters from our country, even though Bessarabia didn't exist anymore. And we weren't happy being so far from home. So we three just watched. We didn't enjoy ourselves.

Finally we asked our Bulgarian friend, "Would you take us to the nearest German village in your wagon? We're really tired. We'll pay you."

"Sure, but first I have a friend; we have to see him first."

So we went, and we had to have a drink. Then another friend. And another drink. And yet another friend and a drink. And so on. These guys really were friends — only not for us. But we had to go along anyway. It was almost dark when we finally left the last one.

After five miles, there was another Bulgarian village. "We can't go by; my friend lives there. I have to visit him."

Then it was midnight, and it would be fifteen miles more before we would get to the first German village.

We Meet the Russians

From all the wine and the lateness, we fell asleep. The horses kept going. Then a rumbling woke me. One wagon wheel went off the edge of the road. The wagon tipped over, and we all fell into the ditch. While we were putting the wagon back onto the road, we saw lights coming in the distance.

We thought, " This isn't safe. We're deserters, and we have no light, so they can see us before we can see who they are." So we turned off into a rock quarry that was luckily right there. We'd hide and let the traffic pass.

Dimitri and I stayed by the wagon. Dompert and Sawall took the horses behind some rocks. That was so the horses' snorting wouldn't give us away.

It turned out to be two Russian tanks. They stopped right there on the road. Then they came into the entrance to the quarry, too. We had gone about a hundred yards in, but had we known they would stop, we could have gone farther back. Now it was too late.

We heard them talking and talking. Then it was quiet. It looked like they would stay all night.

But you know, horses can't keep quiet like people. They kept making little noises. All of a sudden the tanks fired their machine guns at us. I jumped out of the wagon and hid, while the horses went wild and ran off.

Then it was quiet. I figured the other three guys must be shot, because I couldn't see or hear them anywhere. I just crawled farther away from the wagon. I found a drop-off where I was screened from the tanks. Then I could walk. But it was dark and I fell down in a hole, and then another one — holes where they took the stones out. As I was crawling out of the last hole and my head was level with the ground, something moved. I froze. Then I recognized Dimitri's cap, it was my friend!

So we crawled along together until we came to a grain field. We lay down. Everything was quiet. But it got light real quickly. At that time of year, it got light at 3:30 or 4 a.m. And there was a thunderstorm and lightning.

Then Dimitri said, "I have to get the horses and wagon, or else my Daddy will kill me."

What to do? Go back to the Russians, or go away? I had my Romanian uniform on, and they might shoot first. But we had to get the wagon.

I decided, "Okay, let's see the Russians."

We went back along the road, and turned into the quarry.

The tanks got bigger and bigger. Finally the lid of one opened, and a Russian officer appeared—he had two stars on. I explained it was us he heard in the night. Then we went over to the wagon. The bullets had gone through the top of the wagon. We could see the holes. But we found no horses and no harnesses. At least they hadn't been killed.

Dimitri was a good friend from my unit. He was twenty-four years old just like I was, and I felt I had to help him. So we spent most of the day, and we finally found the horses, one here and one there. But no harness was to be found. So I told him, "Okay, here is all the money I have, and you can have my boots."

It was now five o'clock, and I started walking homeward. The rain all day had soaked me through. That and my bare feet made me the picture of a defeated soldier.

After a few miles I saw troops coming. Cavalry. So they couldn't be Romanian. They would be Russians! I could have tried to hide in a cornfield. But if they saw me already, I'd be in worse trouble trying to hide. So I'd best act friendly toward them.

"*Drastite, Tovarichi.*" (Greetings, Comrades.)
"Where are you going?"
"I want to go home."
"Yes, go on home," they told me.

Next I met Russian infantry marching. My heart pounded. But the same thing happened. They wished me a good arrival home.

I was tired, hungry, and thirsty, but I kept walking. It was late evening as I came into a village, the last of the Bulgarian villages. I saw an old Bulgarian woman standing in front of her house.

"Could you spare a small piece of bread?"
"Of course, my poor soldier."

I thanked her warmly. From now on, we Bessarabians were all in the same boat, whether Bulgarian, German, or Romanian.

In that village lived three more comrades from my unit. I looked for one where I could stay. I thought his father was pretty wealthy; he owned a few houses. In any event, you had to have some property, to bring your own horse for service in the cavalry. Sure enough, my friend told me, "You can sleep in our house next door. It's empty."

Next morning after I woke up, I saw more Russian troops. They were marching into the village. Young children greeted them with flowers. It made me feel bad.

Foreboding

I knew how the communists treated their people. We were so close to the Russian border that news from Odessa came over. I remembered a family by the name of Hein escaped over the Dniester. I didn't pay much attention at the time, but then my family talked about it a lot. The Soviets took everything away from the farmers. They sent the men and grown boys to the Arctic or Siberia, to penal camps—never to be seen again. Sometimes they sent the whole family to Siberia. That's why people fled. Many of the German farmers were big landowners, so all Germans were hated.

We heard how the people over there had nothing to eat. If they had a garden, the Soviets took even that away. People were reduced to eating soups made from cowhides or sheepskins and from weeds growing wild.

This "Harvest of Sorrow" was only recently documented in some detail in a book by Robert Conquest. In 1932-33 alone, Stalin and the Communist Party leadership had exterminated some five million peasants in the Ukraine—just across the border from Bessarabia.

The terror actually started at the time of the Russian Civil War. The Bolsheviks used violence and forcibly requisitioned food from the peasants. The ethnic German peasants were especially maltreated as former (World War I) enemies of Russia and as people mostly unenthusiastic about communism. But most of the people who suffered were not ethnic Germans. Altogether, an estimated five million died of starvation in the Soviet Union at that time. Consequently, Lenin had to institute the New Economic Plan of 1921. Peasants were once more allowed to hold individual plots of land.

Harvests were back to normal by 1928, when Stalin decided to communize agriculture and industrialize Russia simultaneously.

Peasants reluctant to join the collective farms faced violence and deportation to the Gulag. At the same time, Stalin ordered millions of tons of wheat a year exported. This would get the foreign exchange credits needed to buy industrial goods and turn the Soviet Union into an industrial power overnight.

Conservative estimates show a total of 14.5 million peasants dying in the Soviet Union from 1930 to 1937 as a result of Stalin's program — 11 million peasant deaths directly from the famine and violence and 3.5 million deaths from deportation to penal camps.

Stalin had his greatest success against the Ukrainian people living across the Dniester River from Bessarabia. The Ukraine had long been a major component of the Russian Empire, but it still had an independent cultural tradition. So Stalin used starvation to stamp out Ukrainian nationalist opposition to the Russian domination of the Soviet Union.

There is clear evidence that Stalin's action was a planned genocide. Peasants bringing back bread, potatoes, or flour from other Soviet Republics had their food taken away at the Ukrainian border. High Soviet officials told the peasants that they would report the food shortages to Moscow and get famine relief, but none was forthcoming. Relief organizations in the West were not allowed to help. Stalin declared that there was no problem. The "internal passport" introduced in December, 1932, prevented peasants from fleeing to a city or anywhere else.

The Ukrainians, as well as other minorities living in the Ukraine, such as the Germans along the Black Sea, were reduced to eating bark, grass, and leather. In some cases, they ate the bodies of others who had already starved to death.

The genocidal actions of 1930–33 had a further effect. The psychological hardening of the Soviet officials who carried out Stalin's murderous orders continued to affect people for a generation. Nikolai Bukharin, a major communist theoretician eventually murdered on Stalin's orders, lamented:

> deep changes in the psychological outlook of those Communists who participated in this campaign and, [who] instead of going mad, became professional bureaucrats for whom terror was henceforth a normal method of administration...a real dehumanization of the people working in the Soviet apparatus (Conquest, 343).

Immanuel recalls:

When I saw the Bulgarian villagers greeting the Soviets that morning, I felt so bad I didn't even have the heart to say goodbye to my friend. I just left. I just started walking.

Finally, at midday, I got to the first German village, Katzbach, where my two friends lived. Dompert's house was right across from the village courthouse, and there I learned he and Sawall got back all right. His father phoned from the courthouse to tell my brother to come and meet us halfway, because it was still fifteen more miles to my own village.

That was my escape from the Romanian army. You could do the sixty miles by horse and wagon in two days easily, but it took me four days of traveling.

Meanwhile, at home the news somehow got out that I wasn't coming back — that I got killed. Johanna was so scared, she went to see her sister, and they visited an old Romanian lady who read cards. When she looked at the cards, she told them they should have heard already: I'm on my way or I'm near. And half an hour later Johanna got the news!

Chapter 3

The Russians Come

It was nice being home again with Johanna and with our girl, Erna, who was a year and a half old then. But the political situation was extremely tense. The war had been on since September, 1939. Poland had been divided up by the Germans and the Soviets. Now the Soviets were here in Bessarabia. We knew that the communist system didn't allow any free peasants. What would happen to us?

Living under the Soviets

Right away we found there wasn't anything more to buy in the stores. No clothes. Not even salt, pepper, or matches. Nowadays we don't think much of these things, but for us they were important. For example, salt was much used. We didn't have any refrigerators or freezers. Meat layered with salt was put in a stone crock or wood tub. It could keep for a long time that way. You just had to soak the salt out before cooking. Pepper was important, along with salt, in making smoked wurst and ham, as well as bacon. That meat would then stay good for the whole summer.

It was summertime when the Russians came, and not a good time to butcher animals. But without salt, it was just about impossible. Any meat not eaten in a day or two would spoil. We had cattle, pigs, and sheep, but we couldn't slaughter them. Maybe the Russians arranged the shortage of salt and pepper for that reason.

We wondered what the people in the cities did if there was nothing to buy. On the land, we had our own vegetables and our own wheat to make into flour. We had meat, too. We killed a lamb and shared the meat with a neighbor. Then, the neighbor

31

killed a lamb and shared the meat with us. And we had chickens and eggs and so on.

We didn't know what was happening in the cities because we had no city newspaper. We had our own German newspaper for our farm villages, but nothing else. And the radio—we weren't supposed to listen, except for stations from Russia. We were pretty much cut off.

Then the command came that we were to report to a neighboring village. There they had big caterpillar tractors to build an airfield. But we had to work there only two days. Maybe they didn't want us to learn too much about what was being built.

The Russian soldiers also made people sell their things to them. My wife Johanna's sewing machine was a wedding present, and it was almost new. Two Russian soldiers tried to buy it from us.

"Too much," they said when they heard it was worth 10,000 *lei* ($62.50 U.S. dollars, the 1935–40 exchange rate). They got mad and they could have done anything to us. I called my older brother who spoke perfect Russian. He convinced them to pay after we added our bike to the sewing machine.

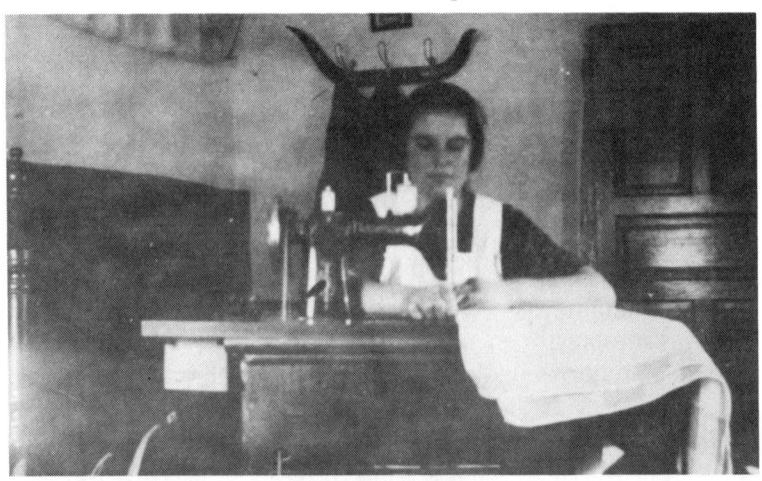

Johanna makes use of the wedding gift coveted by and sold to Soviet soldiers.

Now the grain was ready for harvest—wheat, barley, and oats. We threshed and it was a very good harvest; we thought we were in good shape for the next year. But the order came down, the state was requisitioning a big proportion of our harvest. If they really took as much as they said, there wouldn't even be enough left over for us and the animals to survive till the next harvest.

After I brought in a wagonload of barley, I showed the delivery receipt to the Russian commandant, the commissar. "Where am I going to get paid for this grain?"

"The grain that you must supply is the property of the state. Whatever you have left will belong to you."

I calculated out what they wanted and figured we wouldn't have anything left. We'd even have to give up our animals to the state. They wanted everything. That was their goal, in fact, to make us into employees of a state farm; and those who wouldn't — to Siberia!

Then they commanded that we plow up a third of our fields and sow winter grain. We did what they ordered. We just plowed the crops under. And while we were plowing, the other crops, the corn and soybeans just spoiled out in the fields. Same thing for the grapes and wine-making. Everything just spoiled. But what hurt most of all, we weren't free peasants anymore.

Help from Germany

Around this time, we heard rumors that Germany would take us into their country. They might rescue us from Stalin. We didn't know anything for certain. But if it came to pass, we'd have to show that we were really German. So everyone in the village got to work on their *Stammbaum* (family tree) to show that somewhere way back, their ancestors originally came from Germany.

Actually it wasn't difficult to prove. Our church records had everything. The family tree also had to be certified by a pastor. That, too, was no problem, because our pastors and our churches were still German and private. The state records in the courthouse were either Russian, from before 1918, or Romanian, after 1918, but the German records in the churches saved us.

Hitler's offer to save the Bessarabian Germans was part of a larger plan for the **Volksdeutsch**, or ethnic Germans, first broached in his speech of October 6, 1939, only eight days after the German-Soviet agreement on how they would divide up their Polish gains. Hitler saw that he would need German settlers to bolster the minority German population in the lands annexed from Poland. In addition, Hitler would have to appease Stalin by getting the German minorities out of Stalin's new annexations — initially, Polish Galicia and Volhynia, and in 1940, the remaining territories allotted to Stalin in the German-Soviet non-aggression pact — first, Latvia, Estonia, and Lithuania, and later that year, Romanian Bukovina and Bessarabia. The two problems dovetailed nicely — Hitler needed to populate his new gains with the right kind of people while Stalin's new acquisitions included suspect, possibly troublesome minorities whom he wanted out.

The Germans knew from their secret agreement with the Soviets that the turn of the Bessarabian Germans would come soon, so they had started planning for the repatriation in May 1940, even before the Soviet invasion. Active negotiations with the Soviets took place from the twenty-second of July until the fifth of September. The final agreement closely followed an earlier one made in preparation for the Soviet occupation of the Baltic nations of Estonia, Latvia, and Lithuania as well as for the Soviet occupation of the eastern half of Poland. However, the agreement for Bessarabia went into greater detail, to avoid some of the problems the Soviets and Germans had in the earlier repatriations. They specified what luggage the Germans could take out, the procedure for evaluating and compensating for property left behind, the staffing permitted the German relocation organization, the routes permitted the transports, and so on.

Governmental reports list 93,329 Germans repatriated from Bessarabia. This was more than the number of ethnic Germans recorded as living in Bessarabia. Perhaps some non-Germans were able to pass themselves off as having German ancestors. On the other hand, a 1941 census showed 2,058 ethnic Germans still living in Bessarabia. In any event, roughly 98 percent of the ethnic Germans chose to leave and only 2 percent chose to remain in their homes.

I've heard of only one Bessarabian family who decided to remain behind, a relative of the husband of Johanna's cousin — we don't know anyone else who didn't come out. Johanna's cousin lives in East Germany, so she was allowed to visit the Soviet Union in 1977. The people live ten miles north of our old village, so her cousin visited there, too. But even she had to sneak the visit, because her permit was only for Moldavia — that's what the Russians call Bessarabia now — and our village and the villages south of there are now attached to the Ukraine.

The rest of us — those in West Germany or in this country — don't stand a chance of visiting our homeland. The Russians won't give us visas. The injustice of it all. Russians can visit America or Germany, but we can't go into Russia to see our homes, to see where we were born. We can't even lay some flowers on our mothers' and fathers' graves — God protect them.

Anyway, about the fifteenth of September, four men arrived — a chauffeur and three officers in blue uniforms showing they were in the SS. Everybody was jubilant. We were saved! Everyone in our village registered for resettlement — one hundred percent, even the family where a German girl was married to a Bulgarian boy. Who wanted to live under the communists where they took everything away?

We would have to leave our house and all our things and the lands we had farmed so many years. It wasn't easy to leave everything that our ancestors had built up over 125 years. But it was better to be free!

All our property was evaluated — land, house, farm buildings, animals, machinery, as well as crops. We would be compensated. They said Russia would pay for whatever we left behind.

Then the German soldiers spoke Russian with two Russians who came — one a soldier and the other in civilian clothes. The Germans had brought all the papers and materials that were needed for their work. The Russians even had to use German paper and ink!

In less than two weeks, working day and night, everyone was registered and everything was evaluated. They wanted us out before winter. We had no good roads in Bessarabia. When the rains began, the roads would no longer be passable for cars or buses.

35

Communist Tricks

The process wasn't all smooth though. There were some heated discussions about the property values. We later heard the German resettlement commission had to stay five weeks extra to get the Russians to agree on values. The Russians didn't want to pay for things like buildings, only animals, machines, and other movable things. I heard the Russians finally signed the agreement — after a big drinking party.

The Russians also kept some of the rich Germans, the ones who had a thousand acres or so. Some of them had been officers in the Tsar's army; the Russians killed almost all of those. For example, there was Hoffmann. He was an older man who owned so many buildings, his place looked like a whole village. When we left to go to Germany, the wagons had to go past the courthouse.

"Gospodin Hoffmann," the Russians called, "there is a paper you have to sign."

There were 100 or 150 people waiting for him to come out again. But he didn't come out. So finally some people went into the courthouse. There was no Hoffmann. The Russians took him out the back door to a car and to Akkermann, the county seat.

Later we heard the Germans traced him to Russia, and after six months they got him out. He was lucky he wasn't killed. People like me, the Russians didn't care so much about. They wanted the big land owners and army officers and officials who remembered what it was like during the Tsar's time, before the communists took power.

They especially wanted the ones who fought against communism — in 1918 and 1919, and also a few years later when the communists came over the Dniester to Bessarabia and started an uprising in Tatar-Bunar. Many German farmers volunteered and fought along with officers who used to be in the Tsar's army, including officers like Hoffmann. The Tatar-Bunar uprising was defeated, but the communists still remembered Hoffmann when they came back years later.

The communists don't care for people — like the time we went to East Germany in 1977. We had to report to the police. There they asked, "When did you come in? Look here, your passport is stamped '1971.' " They had stamped the wrong year at the border.

"Your people did that," I told him. He didn't like to hear that, but what can you do? You can't keep quiet.

"You wait here." He got on the phone. After a long time he told me, "It's all straightened out, but if anything more happens, you're in trouble!"

They can be cruel over there, like when we were on the train, and the border police came through to check what we had. "Just our suitcases up there," we told them. But they looked under the seat, pulled the cushions apart, and everything. We had to get out while they searched everything.

The women police did the searching. One squeezed past me in the corridor and pushed her full front up against me. In West Germany or America, I might joke with her, put my arms around her and say, "I won't let you go." But there I think they were provoking me. I didn't do a thing.

Refugees

We lived three months under the communists in Bessarabia. That was enough. On the second of October, 1940, about thirty or forty buses came to our village. In two trips on the next day, they brought the women and children and older men to Galatz on the Danube. The able-bodied men stayed behind. We'd leave on the sixth, using one wagon per family.

We could take only fifty kilos (110 lbs.) with us. Everything else remained behind—house, animals, food, bedding, furniture, and all. I tried to hide some old tsarist silver rubles in our wagon box. But two boys who worked for us knew the hiding place, and the coins disappeared. Some of us were able to take a second team of horses and a wagon. We gave them to a worker, to the pastor, or an official, whoever didn't own a team and wagon themselves. We figured we might get something for them from the Romanians across the river—rather than nothing from the Russians.

The church bell rang for us as we left the village—as we left for the last time. We later learned that the Russians destroyed the church bell and tower afterwards and converted the building to some other use. So 125 years of life, 125 years of work to build up our Bessarabian homeland, was finished.

Galatz was still Romanian territory, and there we gave our wagons and teams to the Romanians. They kept us for a few days — a hundred or more people in each of a dozen tents. Then we sailed up the Danube to Prahova, where the Yugoslav-Germans treated us well. After a few more days, we took a train by way of Austria to Germany, to the refugee camps.

Castle Werneck near Schweinfurt was the camp for people from our village and a neighboring village, two thousand people altogether. It wasn't so nice; we were packed thirty people to a room. The food wasn't so good either. But you had to remember that Germany had been at war for over a year. This was October 1940.

At the camp, they gave us medical exams and shots for I don't know what. They typed our blood and tattooed the blood group (A, AB, B, or O) under the left arm of everyone over fifteen years old. They told us it would make it easier if someone were injured and needed blood.

Then, in November, we were sworn in as naturalized German citizens. Our papers said "O" for *"Osten."* That meant we would get a farm again in the eastern part of Germany.

A precondition for German citizenship had been a special screening by the SD, Sicherheitsdienst *or Security Service of the SS, carried out under the orders of Himmler. "Racially valuable" refugees — conforming to the skull dimensions, etc., of the Aryan race — got an "O" classification. They would be given farms in the eastern territories* ("Osten") *which had been German before World War I and had now been re-annexed from Poland. Those who were marginal in terms of the racial criteria were classified "A" and kept in Germany proper* ("Altreich") *to be workers. Those who were definitely non-Aryan were classified "S" (special) and sent to Poland.*

While we were waiting for resettlement, I worked at a construction company in Schweinfurt. Christmas and New Year's we spent altogether as a village. The Germans had promised that everybody from our village would be resettled together as a village. But it didn't happen.

The wagon train from Kulm leaves Bessarabia, crossing the Prut River into Romania, October 1940.

In February, we were sorted and registered, but not told much. They sent us to Warthegau (German-annexed western Poland). First we went to a transit camp near Litzmanstadt (Lodz) for two weeks. We stayed in nice vacation houses in an evergreen forest, but we were packed in. Then they loaded us on the train again. We came eventually to the small hamlet of Klein Lohe in the district of Kosten, south of Posen (Poznan), to a ninety-acre farmstead with pretty much what we lost in Bessarabia the year before.

In our small village there were just four German families, plus other houses where the hired people lived. We had three hired men on our farm, two older ones and one younger.

We made good progress, although it did take a while until we got used to the new ways of doing things. We cultivated grain — wheat, barley, oats, rye — as well as potatoes, sugar beets, and clover for hay. Our Erna, two and a half when we got there, played with the Polish children and learned the language well. A year after we arrived, in 1942, we had a second girl, Hilma. Everything would have been wonderful if only the war hadn't been on. In the winter of 1942–43, Germany lost 300,000 men at Stalingrad. Because of the losses, many farmers had to become soldiers, me included.

Normal life resumed for the emigrants from Bessarabia during their occupation of the Warthegau villages. The Weisses pause in front of their thatched-roof barn on their way to Sunday church services, 1942.

Chapter 4

Drafted Again

From 1939 to mid–1941, Hitler and Stalin had carved up the small nations of Eastern Europe between them, and Hitler had triumphed in the West, except for Britain. Stalin naturally supported Hitler's attack on Britain by providing shipping and arms — helping Hitler meant that the capitalist powers would not unite against the Soviet Union. But Britain stood fast.

Hitler then turned on his totalitarian comrade in arms, invading the Soviet Union in June 1941. It would be a war in which no quarter would be given, a fight between two unscrupulous powers that would cost tens of millions of lives before it was over. No one in Eastern Europe would remain unaffected, certainly not the Bessarabian–German families resettled on the Eastern frontier of Germany. Immanuel and Johanna would be able to survive only with great luck and by putting to use everything their peasant forbearers had learned about survival.

Historically, the Swabian peasants have had a great deal of experience in surviving wars and conquest by larger nations. In 495 A.D., they were first subjugated by the Franks. Again in the German Peasant War of 1525, they were put down with great bloodshed by the armies of the Swabian nobility and city-states, because Martin Luther had decided that order was preferable to a world turned upside down by the peasants. During the Thirty Years War (1618–1648), Catholic and Protestant armies from all over Europe used Swabia as their primary battlefield and devastated the area so thoroughly that only an estimated 10 percent of the population remained.

At the beginning of the nineteenth century, Napoleon occupied Württemberg and forced Duke Frederick II to supply him with thirteen thousand men. Napoleon placed these soldiers at the head of his troops on the march to the gates of Moscow. Only three hundred survived and returned home alive. *Prussia's victory over Württemberg in 1866 was far less bloody, but like most Swabian peasant experience with the military, the moral would seem to be, "If you want to survive, keep your head down, and don't volunteer for anything."*

Hitler invaded Russia in June 1941, anticipating that the Blitzkrieg (lightning-war) would destroy the bulk of the Red Army and capture Moscow before winter, forcing the Soviets to capitulate. But the Germans discovered the Soviets had at least 360 divisions, not the 200 of their own intelligence reports. The German army was stopped short of Moscow.

With the return of good weather in 1942, German troops again advanced hundreds of miles, mostly on the southern part of the battle line in the Soviet Union. The Red Army suffered five million casualties in the first fifteen months of the war but bought enough time to regroup and make use of their tremendous reserves. In the winter of 1942–43, the Soviets launched their first major offensive at Stalingrad.

During the summer of 1943, the Soviets pushed the Germans back in both the center and the south. By fall, when Immanuel would finish his military training, only two and a half million German troops were left on the eastern front to fight five and a half million in the Red Army. The winter of 1943–44 would see a new Red Army offensive in the north, aimed at lifting the twenty-nine month siege of Leningrad. As the war turned badly against the German army, they would need all the help they could get, including Immanuel's.

Drafted

It finally happened to me after two years on the new farm in Warthegau. I was drafted into the German Army on March 25, 1943, and sent to Sudauen in East Prussia. We got our uniforms and were sworn in. We had to learn the oath by heart and give it with upraised hand. It went something like this:

"I, soldier so-and-so, with this oath, give myself completely, in the name of God Almighty, with faithfulness, honor, and bravery, for the German Empire and our precious Fatherland. God be with us."

We all knew the oath was proper. We were swearing to defend our country. Now, those who went on to special officer's courses also had to swear to be loyal to Hitler. We didn't have to do that.

But our noncom noticed two young recruits — about eighteen or nineteen years old, who didn't say the oath with the rest of us. He challenged them. Why didn't they repeat the oath with us?

"We don't believe in God. If you mention the name of God, we'd rather not give the oath."

The noncom had served in the Polish and French campaigns and in Russia, too. He had been wounded and had medals for bravery:

"I'll tell you young soldiers something. In the French Campaign, I had soldiers like you under my command. They didn't want to believe in God. The fighting was bad, the shells fell, and machine guns mowed down everything above ground, just like a scythe cuts hay. Then these young soldiers, for the first time, cried out to God for help, and they prayed. Think about that!

"You will be sworn in now and you will give the oath with us, whether you believe in God or not. But just remember, how you decide about God is going to affect your life from now on."

I don't know what eventually became of them. They didn't go with us to France for training. We were mostly older men and married. Maybe they sent them right off to the Russian Front?

We had only two weeks of training in East Prussia. I thought, "If it's all like this, I can stand it." We were light cavalry, just bicycles and motorcycles — they didn't have horses in the German cavalry any more. Actually we trained only on bicycles; there weren't any motorcycles available. They gave us some infantry training, too. But it was easy.

At least half of us were *Volksdeutsch* (ethnic Germans) from Russia, Romania, Hungary, and Yugoslavia. I was only twenty-six, going on twenty-seven; some of the others were up to thirty-six years old. They had drafted all the younger ones in the first years of the war; the older ones they left for last. After all, you think a little more when you're older.

After the light training in the East, they sent us to France, to Baiy and then Poissy and St. Germain, near Paris, for six months more training. It was very good training compared to the Romanian Army — strict, but just, with good treatment.

They said if I wanted, I could get my Romanian rank back—I had been a corporal there. But I wasn't crazy about the offer. The higher up you are, the harder you have to work. So I never got to corporal till near the end of the war. I was mostly a *Gefreiter* (private). They would have sent me to school, too, to be a sergeant. But I didn't want promotions. I just wanted to come back alive.

Doing My Duty

I never volunteered; I just obeyed orders. Two of my boys joined the Army Reserve during the Vietnam War. When another was close to being drafted, I went to the draft board and told them about all the years I fought against communism, but now I was going to do everything to get him out of it. I told them, "I need him on the farm; I've got shrapnel in my leg."

So one of them said, "Yeah, you're in trouble now. You've borrowed money and rented more land, and you won't be able to make your payments."

I told him, "No one ever said anything like that to me before, and no one ever had to sue me for payment." I always made all my payments, and I didn't want to hear that kind of talk.

My boy wanted to be a farmer, not a soldier. But everyone has to do his duty as a citizen, including him. I just didn't want him fighting after all the fighting I did against the communists and after I lost everything on account of it. War is hell. Some days there is a little excitement, but mostly it is hell.

Now, going through the training wouldn't hurt; it would make men of them. They would know what life means—accepting some responsibilities. I say, draft everybody. They should have the training and get it over. That's the way it is in Germany today. A strict training hurts no one, especially nowadays when almost everyone can have whatever their heart desires, when everybody believes he can do whatever he wants, without taking on any responsibility.

Our training in France was finished in September of '43, and we were assigned to fight on the Eastern Front. On the way, we stopped at our training camp in East Prussia for a few weeks' layover. There I got a telegram; our third child, Gerda, had been born. So I applied for leave—but all I could get was four days—actually only two days at home, since the train going and coming used up two days.

I should say that at least soldiers came first in Germany. We got free train passage, and people would compete for the honor of giving up their seats to us. "You have to fight for us," they'd say. I can't to this day understand why soldiers are not treated better here in America—when they are our sons fighting for our country and our freedom.

When I got home for the two-day furlough, it was nighttime, and Johanna woke the the older children. When they saw me by their bed, they asked their mother, "What does Uncle want here? Uncle can go home." That's how well they remembered me after the six months I had been away in France.

Our eldest child, Erna, was now five; the second, Hilma, a year and a half; and now a third girl had been born—what a responsibility! And I had to leave for the Russian Front.

I'll never forget the goodbye at the train station after those two days—nor will Johanna. We thought it might be our last goodbye. But I prayed to the Lord that he allow us to meet again even if we had hard times in-between. We were still young—twenty-seven and twenty-three—and we were healthy and full of energy. The Lord heard—we did survive, and we have been able to work together, to save together, and to get somewhere together—with His help.

Partisans

From camp, they shipped us to the Eastern Front by troop train. First we stopped at Plescau (Pskov, just east of the former Russian border with Latvia) to get our assignment. They would send us wherever they needed replacements. Near Plescau, I heard the first shots of the war—fired by partisans.

The Soviet partisans were comprised of Red Army stragglers overrun in 1941, together with able-bodied peasants. They operated mostly in the north where the forested and swampy terrain provided many more hiding places than the steppe in the south. At night, the Soviets would fly into secluded airstrips with weapons, munitions, and supplies, as well as demolition experts and trainers. By mid-1943, there were more than two-hundred thousand partisans hitting German road and rail traffic with hundreds of demolitions every day.

We were sent a few miles east of Plescau, to Karamischewo. The villages along the railroad were destroyed and empty, but the partisans came out at night and planted mines. When the trains came during the day, they exploded. Our job was to put a stop to it!

We lived in bunkers about a mile and a half apart, twelve bunkers or stations altogether. When it got dark, about 4 p.m., we had to start patrolling. Every half hour, four men left from our bunker. Two men went east, two men went west. In each of the other bunkers they were doing the same thing. We would pass the other patrol halfway and go on to the next bunker, sign in, and then return. At each point—when leaving for the patrol, arriving at the other bunker, leaving there, and returning to our bunker—each time we had to write down our name, the date, and the exact time. It took an hour and a half to go over and back, and we did that as long as it was dark, alternating two hours on duty and two hours off. It didn't get light till late—about 8 a.m.—since this was in December and January.

We walked between the railroad tracks, not outside. The mines were on the outside. If you saw one, you didn't stop. You just kept walking and reported the location later. You would see the magnet stuck to the tracks and also some wires. Stopping would have told the enemy we found something. Better they should think we didn't suspect anything. Later a special demolition team would come with an armored train and take the mines away.

It was a dangerous job. The partisans lay in the woods and brush, and we couldn't see them. They could see us perfectly, but they didn't do anything, not until the supply train came heading for the front. Then they'd explode the mine when the locomotive was right over it. It could take three days until everything was repaired—three days when there'd be no food and ammunition for the front. One night, in our small area, seventy mines were found.

Sometimes the partisans were so cocky they came out and went on the attack. At Christmastime, they attacked our stretch of track, when we'd been replaced by a brand new unit with no experience. Our bunkers were very nice, built of sod with a wooden roof, and with a stove so we could sleep in there. The guys in this new unit were caught inside the bunkers, and seven or eight of them were killed.

The German invasion of 1941 had Leningrad as its main objective in the north. The outskirts of the city were reached that fall. But for two years, the Russians had withstood the German encirclement and siege—until early in 1944, when on the fourteenth of January, the Red Army moved to the offensive, both at Leningrad and a little farther south at Novgorod. The Germans were surprised that the Soviets were strong enough to attack in strength at both points simultaneously. Even worse, several good German divisions had been transferred to repair losses in southern Russia. As a result, the attacking Soviets had a three to one advantage in troops and artillery and a six to one advantage in tanks, self-propelled artillery, and planes.

After five days of fighting, it was clear to the German commanders that they would have to lift their siege of Leningrad and move to a prepared defensive line about fifteen miles back. This straightening of the line would free three divisions. But Hitler refused to allow any withdrawal.

The Soviets continued to attack with success, and Hitler finally gave in. But the German fall–back line was breached because of the forced nature of the retreat. And Hitler refused to consider any further withdrawal:

> *If we go back voluntarily he [the Russians] will not get there with only half his forces. He must bleed himself white on the way. The battle must be fought as far as possible from the German border (Ziemke, 256).*

So instead of withdrawing in an orderly way to another major defensive line prepared for such an eventuality, the Germans were pushed back in great disorder. From the fourteenth to the twenty-ninth of January, the German infantry combat strength of fifty-eight thousand was cut by thirty-five thousand wounded and fourteen thousand killed, and, even with new arrivals, could only be brought back to seventeen thousand men. By the end of January, the German 18th Army was close to collapse. Five percent of all rear echelon troops were hastily made up into special units to reinforce the line. But a new emergency arose when additional Soviet troops suddenly arrived from hundreds of miles to the south and began attacking near Lake Ilmen. Here Immanuel would first meet the Red Army.

We were finally sent to the front in early February of 1944, to a brand new unit, the 368th Grenadier (Infantry) Regiment — *Deutsche Krone*. The unit's name came from the city of Deutsche Krone in Pomerania, just to the north of Wartheland. We arrived at night in a forest somewhere near *Ilmensee* (Lake Ilmen). There we were split up to replace soldiers who had been casualties. While we were marching in the forest, our leader told us, "Be careful, any moment we can be attacked." So we came up to a railroad track — our position in the HKL (*Hauptkampflinie* or main battle line).

This part of the HKL was swampland, and there were almost no bunkers. The water table was so high that it was impossible to keep a bunker dry, except for the ones dug into the railroad embankment. It was cold, and nothing stayed dry. Everyone's arms and legs froze. I froze the ends of my fingers.

The swampy ground kept us from using any heavy weapons, just carbines, rifles, and machine guns. Of course, the Russians weren't able to use heavy guns either. But we had an advantage because we were on the railroad embankment and we could be supplied with food and ammunition by armored train. Their positions were mostly farther out in the swamp and forest.

We were told the Russians were to our left at a railroad station only a half mile away, and in front of us beyond the embankment. It was serious. Every night we took turns in a forward observation post on the other side of the embankment. It was so dark that, even with the snow, you had to depend entirely on your hearing.

On the third or fourth day, our alarm bell went off — a small bell in our bunker connected by wire with the observation post. Like lightning, everyone went to their foxholes where grenades and everything were ready. The Russians attacked. We had good positions, and after an hour things died down.

The next day, five of us had to go into no-man's-land to collect the guns and ammunition from their dead. We found eight dead just by our position alone. We hurried because daylight was fading—and in the twilight I saw two dark spots. I yelled to my sergeant, "He's got binoculars on us!" The binoculars dropped and a machine pistol chattered. But we got covering fire from the railroad embankment and came back okay.

That wasn't the only time I was in no-man's-land. The next day the Russians brought up a big supply of munitions. Six of us had to go out that night and detonate their stores. I'll always remember those hours.

Retreating

After a few days we were pulled back to an area near the city of Dno, and we dug in near a village. It was sunny and more or less quiet, although we heard noises in the distance, over the hill in enemy territory.

At one in the afternoon, we suddenly saw thirteen Soviet *Panzer* (tanks) coming down the road towards us. About half a kilometer away, they split up and started across the fields, six to our left and seven to our right.

Our assignment was to guard the road to Dno, our line of retreat, and we didn't expect to be attacked like this. We were only sixty men at most, with four tanks. We were badly outnumbered.

We contacted our headquarters as the tanks tried to encircle us. In just a few minutes we heard some planes. We were careful not to give ourselves away. First, we had to check whose they were. *Stukas*—ours! So we shot up flares to let them know where we were. The planes circled around once and then all hell broke loose. They dove down to maybe only ten or twenty yards above the ground, and they destroyed every one of the tanks. We were saved—at least for this day!

But that wasn't all. At six o'clock the next morning the whole countryside was full of hundreds of Russian infantry, and the road full of *Panzer* with infantry on them. They must have thought we retreated in the night. So our command was to stay hidden and not fire until the first shot came from the four tanks behind us. We didn't have much hope, the Russians were so thick in front of us. Their tanks got about fifty yards away and then our tanks fired. All of a sudden it was like hell on earth. We all fired nonstop.

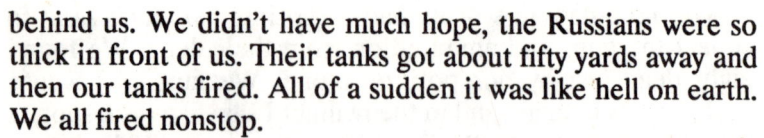

Our tanks hit the first three Russian ones. Their infantry jumped off to both sides of the road. One after another of their tanks was hit and blew up, and the rest turned and fled. We kept shooting at the soldiers until it quieted down. It took three or four hours altogether, because new waves kept coming over the little rise in front of us. The dead lay in their brown uniforms on the snow in hundreds.

That day I had three hand grenades laying ready near my foxhole, when a bullet exploded them. I was lucky, no shrapnel hit me, just lots of gunpowder and dirt blasted into my skin. That's all.

So the afternoon passed. Our sergeant gave the command to hold the position a couple more hours. But how could we? It was getting dark, and we were outnumbered. It was almost six o'clock, and he told us to wait a couple more hours until eight. I wondered if maybe the sergeant had misunderstood and heard eight instead of eighteen-hours (six o'clock, military time). He was from Lithuania.

"If you want to leave now," the sergeant told me, "you'd better go to the command post and ask the lieutenant yourself."

Just then our unit's messenger came and yelled out, "You still haven't left?"

The Russians were only a hundred yards away. It was too dark to see them, but we could hear the voices of their commandos coming. So we took off, and right away one of my comrades—a guy from Baden-Baden—was hit. His leg was blown off. We had a snow-boat—it was five feet long, made of lightweight wood shaped like a boat and used for bringing up ammunition and supplies in the winter, and transporting casualties back. So we pulled him out over the snow.

One person from each group had to stay back and keep shooting while we retreated. I never saw them again.

Earlier, it was I who had to stay behind while the others retreated. You had no choice. You had to obey orders. If not, they would bring you before the *Kriegsgericht* (court-martial).

About a half mile back of us were German troops on snowshoes, and they stopped the Reds. We evacuated the city of Dno and retreated to another city, the name I've forgotten, and rested for several weeks. We had only partisan attacks, but some of them were heavy. We lost some more good men.

Hitler finally accepted a withdrawal when he saw that German troops could be encircled by strong Russian attacks on both flanks. The withdrawal would reduce the length of the front by two-thirds, to the line running north and south through Pskov. By March first, the Germans were behind this prepared defense line of 6000 bunkers and 125 miles of barbed wire. The front stabilized for a while.

Wounded

At the end of March 1944, I again came up to the front. One day during April we were dug into a woods and getting our midday dinner. We got a hot meal once a day. The Russians were in a woods on the other side of the valley, a few hundred yards away. We didn't attack and they didn't attack.

We were in foxholes behind bushes, but we didn't know there were some spots where we could be seen. Maybe they saw the mess containers in our hands and they figured we were concentrated there. In fact we were. Middays, a mess wagon pulled by two horses would come up to our position. One of us would go over and collect seven trays of hot food, another, seven field bottles of coffee for the rest of the comrades.

Going back to my foxhole, I started to take a different way because I wanted to talk to someone. But someone called out, "*Pass auf* (watch out), the Russians see you! There's no cover there." So I disappeared into the woods and went over to the cook-wagon. I filled my bottle with a little more coffee. Suddenly a shell hit about a hundred yards away. Then a second one, closer.

The third one hit right next to the wagon. I went down, hit by shrapnel in the lower legs. The horses were used to firing, but not to a hit five yards away. Maybe they got some shrapnel, too.

Anyway, they bolted. When the Russians saw that, they really started firing.

I couldn't walk, so I just crawled through the foot-deep snow using my elbows. Finally I got far enough away. Our medical corpsman came and cut my boots off and gave me first aid. Then they brought me by wagon to a dressing station in a bunker behind the front. That same night they took me to a hospital where I was operated on. They got everything out except the nine pieces I still carry around in my legs today — shrapnel that sometimes still gives me trouble.

I spent nearly two months recovering in a hospital in Riga, Latvia — till I could walk again. Then I was supposed to have two weeks recovery leave starting the tenth of June. But the sixth of June was D-Day, the invasion in France, and all leaves were cancelled.

My legs weren't really well yet, so I went to the sergeant, a friend of mine, to ask if he could do anything for me, "Do you have a job for me here in the hospital?"

"No."

Well, he liked whiskey, and I didn't drink much, so I told him, "I got a few bottles for you."

Next day he said, "There is a rehabilitation section, where soldiers recovering from their wounds have to exercise. You can take care of the exercise equipment — set it up, put it away."

That lasted only a few days. They told me, "The job is discontinued. If you want to stay here, the only thing you can do is be a helper in the hospital, moving patients, getting drinks of water, bringing meals, helping with the bedpans."

I didn't want to have anything to do with sick people — it was the last thing I wanted to do. But there was no alternative. "Okay, I'm going to do it."

So that was my job. The hospital was a three-story school in Riga. I was ordered to the lower hall where they had sixty-two beds. There was heavy fighting, and the front was getting closer and closer. At night, the transports would come and fill all the beds, there were so many wounded. The doctors sorted them. The ones with bad wounds were sent to Germany, and those with light wounds to another place nearby. Days we would get the place cleaned up and ready for the next night.

There were two nurses and another helper besides me. All day long, for ten or twelve hours, it was go, go, go. After a week or two, I finally liked it there. You could see the gratitude of the wounded in their faces or eyes. They were really helpless. And then someone might say, "I want to write a letter to my mother, to my wife," and I felt really good that I helped him. It was a very responsible job.

Then I was taken onto the regular hospital staff. But at the beginning of July, we got the command that we should pack everything. They said, "We're not gonna get any more wounded; the unit is moving to Germany." The head doctor was a major – he was very good, and he checked me over. I had over-worked, and my wounds had opened again. So they couldn't send me to the front like the healthy ones. "I guess we'll take you along to Germany," he told me and a couple of others.

Back to Germany

In East Prussia, they put us in another hospital because we were still not healed—five of us in one room. It was July eighteenth. We had a few drinks to celebrate being in Germany again. Some nurses were there and we were having a good time.

Suddenly some officers came. They made everyone stand at the end of his bed. They started with the other guys. "What's wrong with you? You look like you'll be ready in two weeks—so you stay here. We'll send you to the front after that."

Another was going to take a long time to heal. "We'll send you back to Germany."

And so it went until me; I was the last. I had nothing serious, just an open leg wound.

"All right, you stay here, and then to the front."

"That's not very good news for me on my birthday," I told them.

"Oh? Your birthday? Let's check your *Soldbuch* (service book). Okay, *verlegt* (postponed)."

So they sent me to Oberhof, Thüringen, and I spent another month there recovering at a sanatorium. After a few weeks, Johanna was able to visit me for three days. But shortly after that I got an order that the leave I had been promised was canceled.

So I went to the commander and told him I was a farmer and I hadn't been home for over a year to take care of all the work, Johanna was on the farm alone with foreign workers, and so on. He called his clerk and commanded, "This man gets two weeks recuperation leave and two weeks work leave — immediately."

It was nice to be home with the family and to take care of all the work. But naturally it didn't help my leg at all. It got worse and the wound broke open again. Well, my four weeks were up and I had to report to the *Deutsche Krone* (368th Infantry Regiment) again.

I learned that many of my buddies — the ones I had trained with in France so long ago — had been lost on the Eastern Front while I was recovering from my wounds. They had had to stop retreating at some river, and they had been in a battle for a long time.

I prayed. I didn't want to treat anyone wrong; I just wanted to survive. I prayed a lot. Maybe that's why I survived.

Then I was sent to Deutsche Krone, Pomerania, to the marching company of my unit, where we had exercises every day. My leg wasn't healed completely, so I had to see the doctor. Because the hospital was full, he gave me a special permit that let me stay in my bunk, where I could get bed rest.

Well, the whole company was out marching the next day when the *Hauptfeldwebel* (the head sergeant) came in to where I was in my bunk.

"What are you doing?" he yelled.

When I told him I was lying in bed, he gave me such a sarcastic response. "Getting comfortable! I never saw such a thing. This never happened before."

Then I showed him the special permit from the doctor. He couldn't do anything. But when he saw me again the next day, he told me such a thing was not permitted — for someone to be in quarters and in bed during the daytime.

Sure enough, orders came down that men not able to march would be reassigned. The lieutenant told me, "We'll send you to an antitank unit. They're motorized there."

That was okay with me. I thought, "Every day I have to train makes the war shorter for me."

So, starting in October of 1944, I spent five weeks in Kolberg on the Baltic training on the 3.7 cm., 5 cm., and 7.5 cm. PAK

(*Panzerabwehrkanone* or antitank guns). These were *direktschuss* (direct-shooting). You wouldn't fire at the tanks from behind a hill. You had to wait until you could see them directly. Then I had two weeks *Einsatzurlaub* (special leave) because this was a new unit for me. It was still the *Deutsche Krone*, my old 368th Infantry Regiment, but the 14th Company, the heavy company with tanks.

When I came back from the leave, I found almost all my new comrades gone. Only a few were left.

"Weiss, where were you? Your name was on the blackboard..." — that was where they listed the new assignments — "...to go to the Russian Front."

"I was on leave. No one called me."

"Well, you sure were lucky."

As Christmas of 1944 passed quietly in camp, I knew I'd be sent somewhere soon — but where? Every morning I checked the blackboard.

Chapter 5

On the Western Front

The Western Allies landed in Normandy on the sixth of June, 1944, while Immanuel was still recuperating in Riga. They broke out and liberated Paris in August, and by September reached the German border. Allied troops took the German city of Aachen in October, and in November liberated Antwerp in Belgium to provide major port facilities. Hitler decided to contest every foot of German territory instead of withdrawing behind the easily defensible Rhine River. American troops concentrated in the area of Aachen and moved toward the Rhine in bloody fighting during November.

Hitler then launched a surprise offensive across the rough terrain of the Ardennes to recapture Antwerp. The Battle of the Bulge began on December sixteenth with great initial success for the Nazis, but it ultimately failed. The Germans lost a quarter million troops and six hundred tanks and assault guns. It took the Allies only about six weeks — until the end of January — to recoup the ground they lost.

On the second of January, 1945, my name came up with four or five others. We were to be sent to the Western Front. I knew I had to go, and I was happy that it was in the West. I knew some day soon the war would be over, and on the Western Front there was some chance to live. If I survived the fighting and was captured, I'd be dealing with Christians.

Retreating

We went through Köln (Cologne), where we were bombed, and then to Huchelhofen, near Aachen, to fight against the English. It was really quiet. We lived in cellars because the houses were all shot up. The walls had big holes and you could

57

still see clothes, featherbeds, clocks, kitchen pots and pans, all kinds of things. The people had to leave so quickly, they took only food. No people were left in the village. How miserable to see the destruction where the shells smashed in the walls. We went from village to village, and it was all the same.

We were thrown in wherever they needed troops. We were supposed to use the antitank guns we trained on, but the 3.7 cm. PAK was too light for the tank armor the enemy had. (The 3.7 cm. PAK was almost ten years old at this point.) And there weren't many 5 cm. or 7.5 cm. guns available. So they gave me an *Ofenrohr* (rocket launcher) for close combat with tanks. I was gunner number one while gunner number two carried the rockets for me. We were supposed to stay in the background until the enemy tanks appeared.

The fighting was light. We knew there was no use fighting. If we were attacked, we would fight. If not attacked, we'd move back slowly.

We were in one place for a week, and then there was a firefight. Finally a white flag went up. We went out to get our wounded and the British got theirs. We never saw this before, not in Russia. When you were wounded there, you either got help from your buddies right then or it was curtains for you.

From the twenty-second to the twenty-fourth of January, we were under continuous artillery fire, living in the cellars, cold and hungry. We knew little about the front in the East. But whenever I could, I would go over to our command post to figure out where the front had gotten to. I could see that the fighting was getting close to Warthegau and my family.

Our company head, a young lieutenant from Vienna, a nice man, knew that my home was near Posen. One evening he came to my post, excused me, and brought me to our little bunker in the trenches. We had a small stove and a sack over the door to keep it a little warm. He brought me into our little hole with its dim candle. I could see he wanted to say something, but as kindly as he could.

After a while he told me, "Posen has been overrun by the Russians. Army reports say the civilian population has been evacuated. I just wanted to make sure you know that."

So I had lost my home again. This injustice sticks with me to this day—people are driven out just because they belong to a certain nationality. I hold not only the government in Berlin to blame for that, but the governments in Moscow, Washington, and London, too.

Some days later, I got a postcard from Johanna saying they were in Cottbus and still heading westward. So they had left home before the Russians got there.

But I heard nothing more. Shortly afterwards, we were dispersed by an attack and I had to join another unit. So I thought, maybe they wrote again, but the mail got lost on the way. And I couldn't get in touch with them because they were still fleeing ahead of the Russians — I hoped.

We were always retreating — I can't describe where we went. Life; the future had no more meaning for me. It was especially bad for us soldiers whose *Heimat* (homeland) was in the East. Our families were lost, and there we were. We asked ourselves, "Was life still worth living under these conditions?"

I think most German troops at that time felt there was no purpose in fighting — "We can't stand and fight half the world." And we remembered the German saying, "Many rabbits have been killed by dogs even when the rabbit is still healthy and able to run fast."

But life went on — you had to have hope, to take hold with new courage. We said to ourselves, "The Americans and the British will occupy Germany and protect us from the Russians." Of course, we didn't know that Germany had already been divided up at Yalta.

Once, around the twelfth of March or so, we had some tanks with us — ten or twelve, to try to throw the British back. But we had to keep retreating toward the Rhine. I think we were somewhere east of Düsseldorf.

It got real bad when we were backed up to the Rhine. They were shooting at us all the time. I was assigned to be messenger — very dangerous. I had to go from one command post to the next bringing reports. The telephone wires didn't last long; they were shot up so quick.

Then, one evening I got a special assignment: with eleven men, hold the Hans Kniepe Bridge over the Rhine until 2000 hours (8 p.m.) so our vehicles could get across. It was a railroad bridge with planks laid around the rails so vehicles could drive across.

We set up the defense. Everything went all right until 2000, so we moved back to cross over. But the whole bridge was still full of trucks. Some had been hit and they blocked the others. The shells were exploding over us, in front of us, and in back of us. We crept under the trucks, climbed over the trucks. Anything to get over to the east bank of the river.

On the way over I got hit with shrapnel again on my right leg. I couldn't go on. One of my buddies in back of me, a guy from Hamburg, helped me over to the other side.

The wound wasn't very bad. The shrapnel didn't have much power behind it. So after a week in a military hospital, I was on my feet again.

After that, we didn't get in any battles for a while. We just kept moving back. But we didn't talk about surrender, either. We were strangers; we didn't know if we could trust each other.

The people from the other side of the Rhine had been evacuated along with us. So when we were in a village north of Osnabrück, some of the local people invited us for dinner on Easter Monday, the ninth of April. Shortly before midday we got to their house and everything was normal. There were no signs of getting ready for evacuation. They even had Adolf's picture up yet.

Suddenly, the command came, "The English are at the edge of the village — we must give up the village."

So we moved out to a woods where we could dig foxholes. We could see the English, about a mile and a half away. It got toward evening, and our lieutenant sent a messenger: "My headquarters is a quarter of a mile away from you, in the farmhouse. The messenger will bring commands."

We waited, but no commands came. It got dark, and everybody fell asleep. Next morning we thought something was wrong. Still no messenger. So we eleven men walked over and asked the farmer about our lieutenant.

"He left yesterday. The English were here yesterday, too."

And we learned the English had gotten around behind us, too. So we knew we had a problem. The farmer gave us a piece of bread, some milk, and some advice: "Be prepared to run into the English."

He had an open building with some straw stored there, so we sat down and decided what to do. I joked, "In case we need it, I have a white handkerchief."

Prisoner of War

Then we walked down the farmer's lane toward the road, and we could see soldiers moving back and forth. When we got closer, they started firing at us. I took out my handkerchief. I was ahead of the others, so the British came up to me first. They took my wrist watch, rifle, ammo belt, pistol, and my food. The others, fifty feet behind me, got the same treatment. But they were allowed to keep their food—which was important.

So we were lined up—they had many prisoners already, maybe 100 or 150. We were marched through the village we were forced to leave earlier. The mother and two girls who invited us for Easter dinner were there and saw us. But nobody could do anything for us. We were prisoners.

We were taken to an open, sixty-acre field full of prisoners. There was no protection from the rain that came down day-and-night. Eventually we were so tired, we lay down on the cold wet ground. We just brushed the water and mud away, laid one coat on the ground, and used another coat as a cover. We were two men together, lying on our sides, first one side and then the other, to keep a little warm.

There was hardly anything to eat or drink. A truck came with a big barrel of water and we all ran for it. Whoever pushed in got some water. But for four or five days, all the food I got was ten crackers a day.

Then a group of us, one from each unit, was taken away to a barn where intelligence was going to talk to us, find out how strong our units were and so on. While we were waiting, some of the British ate bread and other things right in front of us. But a couple of other soldiers first looked each way and then threw us some bread. That's how different some people can be! I never did get interviewed by intelligence.

From there, we were taken by train through Holland to Belgium. We had to watch out because the people threw rocks at us. We were in unprotected, open railcars without any roofs. People stood on bridges and poured boiling water and other things on us.

We were taken off at Waterloo and arranged in rows of six men each, and marched through the town. Civilians threw big rocks and water on us from the upper stories of buildings. On

61

our left we had Belgian guards who hit us with their bayonets. I saw them shoot a guy who fell out of line from weakness. The English on our right were just the opposite—very proper, and they protected us.

They gave us some food at the POW camp, but not much. One loaf of bread, eight or ten inches round and three inches thick, and a small piece of wurst or butter or cheese. Not even enough for one meal, but it had to feed three of us for a whole day. Finally at the end of May, they started giving us a plate of soup in the evening. That helped. But we were so weak that most of the time we just lay on the ground. When they called for help in the kitchen, peeling potatoes and so on, I volunteered, and life got a little better. The cooks couldn't give us much, only a five-gallon pail of coffee, but it had plenty of cream and sugar. Never in my life did I have coffee that tasted so good.

Our POW camp had sixty thousand men, divided into twenty units of three thousand each. One day on the way back from working in the kitchen, I saw our whole unit standing at attention—in rows ten feet apart and five feet apart in the row. Some were bare from the waist up.

They led our work detail to the back. "Take your jacket and shirt off and wait." There were three English officers, and when they came, you had to raise your hands. Then they said, *"wegtreten."* They sent us back to our tent. I asked my buddies about it—twelve of us were crammed into a tent about fourteen feet square.

"They found two," my tent-master explained.

"Two what?"

"Two SS—with the tattoo, and they took them away." He told how the soldiers were looking under the arms for tattoos.

"They didn't see anything on me." When I checked myself, I saw why. My "AB" blood type wasn't visible anymore. What luck!

I guess the SS had the blood type tattooed under the arm like us Bessarabians. All the men—and women, too—got tattooed in 1940 when we were made naturalized citizens. They used a hot electric needle and some dye and made a tattoo of lots of little dots under the left arm. From 1940 to 1945 my tattoo must have worn off. Otherwise it would have been tough for me.

I helped another guy in the camp with his tattoo. He came from the other side of the Dniester from us—a German from the Ukraine. I took a razor and cut his tattoo out. Whether he was SS, I don't know. I didn't want to ask, because at that time you just didn't want to talk about it. It was bad enough to be a prisoner, without bringing up the word "SS." We had to protect each other. And I knew that towards the end of the war many were taken into the SS without their even being asked. If you were healthy and 5 1/2 feet tall, you were in the SS instead of the army whether you wanted it or not.

One day when our group came to work in the kitchen, a cook came up to us with a big butcher knife in one hand and a newspaper in the other. The paper showed a mass grave in eastern Poland where many Polish soldiers had been shot. The paper must have said that the Germans did it.

"I'm going to kill you all," he yelled.

We couldn't do anything. We couldn't defend ourselves. But finally some guards came between us, and he left us alone. Later, a special commission decided this mass murder was committed by the Russians after they occupied that part of Poland in 1939. Over four thousand Polish officers were buried in a mass grave at Katyn Forest near Smolensk.

In June, they assembled us and asked all farmers to report. That's how I was freed. On the twenty-first of June, I left to help bring in the German harvest.

A hundred of us went back through the same town to the same train station. This time we had only one guard in front and one in back. No one harmed us. People had changed in the two months from April to June. We could hardly believe it. I think what happened was that people had heard about the Potsdam meetings in Germany and the trouble the Russians were giving the West.

While we were in the POW camp, the little news of Germany we got was posted up on a bulletin board. News, for example, that the negotiations with the Russians weren't going so well. We hoped the English and the Americans would get together to drive the Russians out of Germany. But it didn't happen. We were all ready to volunteer and help fight the Russians.

We also had some first-hand contact with the Russians. The unit right next to us had Russians and German Russians; it was an international camp. They yelled across the barbed wire separating us and told how the Soviets came and invited them back to Russia. But few took them up on it.

63

Later on I met Weber again — the man whose tattoo I cut out. He and two other comrades were going into the East Zone. The Russians had invited them back, telling them that their service in the German army was forgiven. Only God knows what happened to them. But I do know that scarcely a single German Russian remained in the Russian Occupation Zone. They were all sent back to Russia against their will. The only exception might be if they were married to an East German citizen. Otherwise, goodbye.

One news item I saw posted on our POW bulletin board quoted Churchill as saying, "We have felled the wrong tree." He meant that Germany was destroyed and Russia and communism made stronger. Just see how communism has spread in the whole world since Germany and Japan were defeated. Now there are Russian submarines along the California coast, not to say inside Swedish harbors. They even shoot down airliners with our people in them, and what do we do?

I came out of the POW camp as a defeated German soldier with only an army uniform to my name, no other belongings. And from our uniforms, they even took our honor — our army rank, our decorations for bravery, our unit patches. I came out with no homeland to go to, and no family either, for all I knew.

Before we were split up and sent to different farmers, the British brought us together in a large building in Hildesheim for a couple of days. The food wasn't fancy, but we got enough — more than just the once-a-day bread and soup.

On the third day, we left for our various farms. Each of the German POWs got 60 *Reichsmarks* ($15 dollars). Those of us who lived in the East — that is, east of the Oder River — got nothing! I guess since Germany lost all that territory, the people who used to live there weren't considered Germans any more. The British decided that those from the eastern part of Germany (Prussia, Pomerania, Silesia, Warthegau) were refugees, not Germans.

I'll never forget when I got to the farm — it was 2 p.m., the twenty-seventh of June, 1945. Right away they called me into the kitchen and they fed me pork chops and red cabbage and gravy. I can still taste it today!

Immanuel was fortunate to be captured by the British and serve only two months as a POW before being released. Some POWs were held by the Soviets for five years in Siberia — those who survived. Some 1.5 million of the 3.5 million German prisoners in the Soviet Union died.

Chapter 6

Flight of the Women and Children

While *Immanuel was fighting and retreating on the Western Front, the Russians were getting closer to the eastern border of Germany and to Immanuel's family. The Germans had retreated to a defensive line running south of Pskov by the end of March, 1944, but the subsequent Russian offensive bypassed most of these German troops in the Baltic states and pushed southeast, reaching almost to Warsaw and, most importantly, the borders of East Prussia. Here the lines stabilized from the end of the summer and into the fall and winter of 1944. Hitler did not want to give up any German soil. The psychological effect on German allies, and on the Germans themselves, would be disastrous.*

For the first time, the refugees on the roads would be citizens of Germany. And those who stayed behind could expect a horrible fate. The German invasion and occupation had cost the Russians twenty million lives. The Germans had been brutal, and now the piper would be paid.

The Germans stabilized their lines, and the Russians did not renew their attacks, not even when the Polish Home Army rose up in Warsaw. But German strength was ebbing quickly—at the southern end of the Eastern front the Russians had cleared Germans from their own country as well as Romania and much of Hungary. Between June and November, the Germans lost 1,457,000 men. In response, Hitler called up the **Volkssturm** *or home guard, made up of boys as young as sixteen and men as old as sixty.*

In January of 1945, the Russians once more took to the offensive in the north. They attacked on the twelfth, more than a week earlier than they had planned, because of Churchill's urging. The Ger-

67

mans had weakened the Western Allies in the Ardennes offensive and a Russian attack would take off some of the pressure.

The Russian troops outnumbered the Germans more than two to one overall. At the points where they attacked, the Russians outnumbered the Germans nine to one. Warsaw fell quickly and the Russians easily broke through the German lines. The Germans hoped to withdraw to a new defensive line at Posen, but the Russians moved quickly—eighty-five to ninety miles between January twentieth and twenty-second alone. It was a Russian Blitzkrieg this time. On the twenty-third, the Soviets reached Posen and by the twenty-fifth the Posen Line had been breached by tanks. Russian forces pushed on to the Oder River, covering up to 250 miles in eighteen days. Berlin was only forty miles away.

German civilians fled in terror. They had heard what happened when the Red Army first reached East Prussia back in October. Along the roads, the Soviets had put up posters reading, "Red Army Soldier: You are now on German soil; the hour of revenge has struck" (Ziemke, 188). Soviet author Ilya Ehrenburg told Red Army troops in a leaflet, "Kill. Nothing in Germany is guiltless, neither the living nor the yet unborn..." (de Zayas, 65). And Alexander Solzhenitzyn recorded, "...all of us knew very well that if the girls were German they could be raped and then shot. This was almost a combat distinction" (Solzhenitzyn, 21).

German troops were able to push the Red Army out of several villages and capitalize on the opportunity for international propaganda about the Soviet atrocities—not realizing the negative effects for their own people. Columns of refugees—women and children—had been run over and squashed flat by Soviet tanks. An observer reported:

> In the first farmyard...stood a wagon made of wooden framing to which four naked women were nailed through the hands and into the shape of crosses... [Farther on] was a barn with two big doors, each with a naked woman, nailed through the hands in the shape of a cross. We found in the houses altogether seventy-two dead women, children, and a man, aged seventy-four, almost all murdered in a bestial fashion, except for the few who were shot in the neck. Some babies had their heads bashed in. In one room, we found an eighty-four-year-old woman sitting on a sofa...half of her

head had been sheared off apparently with an ax or a spade (Schieder, 8).

Such atrocities occurred, of course, in retribution for the war of ethnic extermination which Hitler had waged in the East for years. Hitler had ordered a relatively lenient occupation in the West and, consequently, there had been many collaborators among the French and other nationalities. But the Nazis considered the Slavic peoples subhuman. They were on Hitler's priority list for extinction right behind the Jews. It is estimated that up to thirty-five million died in the war.

Retribution towards the Germans, even innocent ones like Johanna and her children, was not only possible, it was likely. She reports on their life in Wartheland and what happened when the Russians caught up with them:

It was nice to be together as a family on our farm. But Immanuel was drafted in March of 1943. In the five years we'd been married, it seemed we were separated at least half the time — when he was in the Romanian Army and then because of the resettlement program. So I was left again — with two small children.

Life in Wartheland

I was alone with the Polish workers who helped on our ninety-one acre farm. There were also still three German–Bessarabian farmers in the village, but the rest were Poles. We women did our best by the farm work. We felt foreign and alone, abandoned. But some of our hired help were good, and things went all right.

Farmers had to give a certain proportion of everything produced to the government. For example, since we raised pigs, we could slaughter two for ourselves, but the rest we had to deliver to the government. For every laying hen, we had to deliver eighty eggs per year. But we could slaughter chickens and ducks and geese for ourselves, so we could live well. We gave up all of our wheat and rye, and in return were allowed a certain ration of bread.

We planted plenty of potatoes, sixteen to twenty acres. Half were eating potatoes which the government got, to feed the city people. The other half were feed potatoes, not so good-tasting but big-producers. The pigs got those potatoes—after boiling, together with millet or oats. You couldn't feed them only rich food like corn.

We in the countryside always had enough to eat. Other things like clothing and shoes were rationed—we applied for a permit to buy them. The shopping we did by bicycle or with the team and wagon. We were able to go to religious services every Sunday, too, when we wanted to. Nothing stood in the way. In general, we were living almost a normal life again—by the time Immanuel got drafted.

In 1944, we had refugees come to stay in our village—three families from the Ukraine and a woman and two boys from the Crimea. They had to leave everything behind and flee. We pitied them. But soon it happened to us.

Oh, the authorities told us not to worry. The Soviet Army would be driven back. And we didn't want to believe we would have to leave our homes again. "And where to?" we asked ourselves. I guess the authorities didn't want to say anything that would make us all panic. So we waited for commands. What else could we do? A new year came—1945, and things were still well organized, even though we had almost continuous air attacks—bombing of civilians and strafing of the farmers in the fields.

One Saturday evening about the twentieth of January, there was a knocking on my window. I had just bathed the three girls and put them down to sleep.

"Frau Weiss, get ready and go to Karlshausen. The Russians are close. You must be in Karlshausen in two hours."

It was a surprise, because we hadn't heard the sounds of artillery and there were few planes then. And there was no news from the radio because of static interference. We knew that the time would come when we might have to flee, like the refugees on the main highway that passed about four miles from us. But not yet! We still hoped that we might not have to give up everything we owned, everything we knew. Who wouldn't hang on to their *Heimat* (home) till the last moment possible?

So now I had only an hour to get the children and everything ready to leave. We already had a frame on top of our wagon, together with a cloth woven of flax. It was more to keep out the wind — rain would come right through. Our Polish hired hands quickly helped me put the covering over the wagon and helped get some flour and grain together. For food, I took a five-gallon can of milk, some lard, cooked sausages and ham, and all the bread we happened to have. I gathered the most necessary clothing, and very important, two feather beds — one for underneath the children and one for on top, so they were a little protected from the cold. We couldn't take pots and pans or furniture or anything else. There was no room. Most of the space on the wagon was taken up by sacks of oats for the horses and sacks of rye flour for us. Everything else I left behind.

Cows amble in the barnyard of the Weiss home in the village of Klein Lohe near Posen (now Polish Territory) during the German occupation, 1942.

    One woman took her hired man along, and he told her later that my younger hired man had planned to kill me. He was just twenty-two and hated the Germans. When we were getting ready to leave, he asked me to come up to the attic and help hold the sacks while he filled them with the rye. Well, I didn't trust him; I didn't want to be alone with him.
    The ladies, the wives of the hired help, were nice to us. They used to get food from us, and one boy and one girl stayed with us and ate at our table. We treated them as equals and they knew that. The German government said we shouldn't, but we felt if we worked together, we would eat together. That's why these people helped us get ready.

In 1940, the Weisses didn't know what they were getting into by accepting Hitler's offer of help and resettlement. But they seem to have acquitted themselves well, despite the general hatred and hostility the Nazi government encouraged towards the Polish people.

In Immanuel's words: "The German government promised us when we left everything behind in Bessarabia, 'You'll get a farm back in Germany.' When we went to Warthegau, we saw all these people standing around, and I suppose some may have owned the farm we were given, but we didn't know that at the time. We didn't know they were forced to leave."

In the year after the invasion of Poland, some thirty thousand Poles were deported from the German-annexed areas of Wartheland and Danzig-West Prussia. They were cruelly driven out of their homes, often with only minutes' notice, to be sent to the General Government or part of Poland centering on Warsaw and occupied by the German military. By mid-1941, the total number deported was over a million. This process began with the expropriation and expulsion of the large landowners and soon included even the small peasants. By October 1941, some 80 percent of the area annexed by Germany had been confiscated from Polish owners.

Some conflict between Germans and Poles was not new, although this modern effort at conquest surpassed earlier ones in cruelty. In the 1920s, the Poles themselves had confiscated German farms in contravention of the Versailles Treaty protections for the minorities in these areas amputated from the German Reich. But before that, the Prussians had done the same thing to the rural Polish populations in these same areas. In fact, the Prussians — together with the Russians to the east of Poland — had been trying to swallow up the whole of the Polish nation for centuries. But the stubborn and courageous Poles survived this latest attempt to partition their nation. They would eventually come back and could be expected to exact revenge.

Compared to most Germans, Johanna found it relatively easier to flee and leave almost everything behind. She had been living in Wartheland only a few years. Some German families had been living there for several generations. Millions of other Germans in adjacent provinces never gave a thought to leaving their lands —

BESSARABIAN KNIGHT

the Germans living in Silesia, East Brandenburg, Pomerania, and East Prussia. They feared a Russian occupation but assumed they would still be living in Germany. These territories were homogeneous—99 percent German, and had been German for five, six, or more centuries. Many decided to stay.

Still other Germans—the Volksdeutsch or ethnic Germans living as minorities in Czechoslovakia, Hungary, Romania, and Russia, also had to face the question of whether to flee with the retreating German troops. They had lived there for centuries and could not easily give up the homes of their ancestors. On the other hand, some of them had behaved quite arrogantly and even criminally after the Nazis had occupied their countries. Some had remembered when they had been part of Austria-Hungary, when Germans had a protected and dominant status. They felt abused in the years since the dissolution of the Austro-Hungarian Empire and took advantage of the Nazi occupation of their countries to settle scores. Undoubtedly many of this guilty element fled. Unfortunately many of their ethnic German compatriots stayed, perhaps believing their good relations with non-German neighbors, or at least their innocence, would protect them from retribution.

For the Weisses and other Bessarabian Germans in Wartheland, the choice was clear. Their hands may have been for the most part clean—they had no scores to settle with non-German neighbors and they could respect the Polish in the same way they had their Bulgarian neighbors in Bessarabia. But they had no ancestral ties here—this wasn't really "home," and, most importantly, they already knew what it was like to live under a communist occupation.

Fleeing Westward

In Karlshausen, we met people from all around, and we headed our wagons westward. We traveled day and night, stopping only to feed the animals and to sleep a little. Mostly, we kept moving. We didn't want to fall into the hands of the Russians.

The roads were snowy and icy, and it was hard to travel. One side of the road was for us refugees fleeing west. The other half was for troops moving east to the front.

G. F. WIELAND

We were mostly women and children. A neighbor had her boy, Hugo, a soldier, hiding in her wagon. He had been on leave for a few days with a small wound, so he changed into civilian clothes and hid to finish out his leave. If any soldiers were seen on leave, they were taken right to the front. Only the old or severely wounded men were left. But at the end of his leave Hugo put on his uniform and went back to his unit.

It was miserable when something went wrong with a wagon and it had to be shoved off the road and left behind. But everything went on. Everyone had to save themselves as best they could. You know, there were altogether eight million people who fled. So there was no waiting just for a single person.

On the wagon in front of us was a woman with many children. She would walk to keep warm. When she couldn't walk any more, she'd sit on the wagon. No one knows if she fell asleep or what, but she fell on the road. Dead. Her children cried so. But she had to be left. Everyone had to keep going. Many people were left dead on the side of the road like that—some covered with a cloth, some just lying there.

Frau Krämer, a neighbor and friend from Klein Lohe, came along with me on the wagon. She was a refugee from Odessa in the Ukraine. Her life in Soviet Russia had been awful. Her husband had been taken away by the Bolsheviks, the fate of many German people during the 1930s. For one reason or another, German peasants were enemies of the state. Then in 1939–40, those men still left at home were taken away to build defensive fortifications. We know someone here in America who was able to come out from the Kuban (northern Caucasus), but most of the German-Russian men ended up like Frau Krämer's husband, never heard from again.

Her two children were seven and nine years old, while my three were seven, three, and one-and-a-half at the time. The children kept each other warm under the feather beds. We women took turns driving; otherwise we walked to keep warm. It was too cold to just sit, one of the coldest winters in a long time. We learned later how, after a child died, a mother took the frozen body along in the wagon, to bury later.

We were able to keep up with our neighbors' wagons for some days. Then all at once, we found we were alone, separated from them. We were scared, but after a while we met my uncle. He had his own problems, too. He was in his fifties and had devoted himself to his invalid wife, my mother's sister: "She's bad. She was sick when we left and she's been lying in the wagon the whole time. I don't know what to do." She died a week or so later.

Even people in the same family sometimes got separated because there were so many people. Children could lose their parents and never find them again. Neighbors of ours from Bessarabia had two girls, thirteen and fifteen, who were sent home from their school to be with their parents as the Russians approached. But the parents had to leave home fast like us. Instead of waiting, they went to the school to get the girls, but they weren't there. The parents had to flee without them.

Years later we learned what happened. They were captured by the Russians and sent to Siberia. Only the thirteen-year-old survived. My brother in Germany went to Moscow and spoke to her by telephone, and some years later she was allowed to visit Germany. She met her parents, but communication was bad — she spoke only Russian. Then she had to go back to Russia because her husband and child couldn't get out.

From time to time on our flight we had to leave the wagon — to look for a sleeping place, feed and water for the horses, or soup for ourselves from an Army field kitchen. Our ground-rule was that the children always had to hold hands while we were gone, so they wouldn't wander off and get lost.

Once in a while, we were lucky enough to stay overnight with good people — when there was still room for us. At least then we could be warm and sleep. And once in a while we also got some warm food. Warmth in any form was a real blessing.

We really pitied our horses. The hard roads wore down their horseshoes, so when there was snow or ice, they slipped and slid all over. And after a while, they got skittish all the time. They never had any real rest and quiet. We had to drive them on and on. When there was a stable, it was a strange one and they couldn't really rest. Besides, they were not used to us women. On the farm, the men always worked them or fed them.

At the beginning of February, we finally stopped in the village of Züllichendorf (near Luckenwalde, thirty miles south of Berlin). The three children and I were assigned a room. At this point the horses were so upset with me that I couldn't feed them any more. The landlord had to do it. Later the German Army took them and we never saw them again. At least we were safe from the Russians, or so we thought.

We lived with a family—a man and woman, their daughter, and their granddaughter. People didn't want to take in refugees, but they were forced to by the German government. That's why there wasn't always a warm feeling, having to live with people they'd rather not. And we paid no rent. We lived for free—because we lost everything from the war—while they were still able to keep something.

Bombed in Berlin

Some time after we arrived in Züllichendorf, I learned that my husband's sister, Elise, had also found refuge in the area, closer to Berlin. So I got a permit from the *Burgomeister* (mayor) allowing her to live in our room. We wouldn't be alone. It would be good, even if we were five in one room.

We took the team and wagon to get her—it would be a three-day trip. I had to take all three children with me; I couldn't leave them with anyone. As we headed toward Berlin, we heard air raid sirens howling all around us. We felt like crawling into the ground, if only a hole would appear. We were on a main road, so we quickly went off into a woods, taking the horses with us.

German troops were in the woods, and they came and told us to lie down for safety. Then we saw the planes, flying low in great masses. We prayed each time we saw more, that they not drop their bombs on us. After some passed over more would come. Then there was a battle in the sky and planes were shot down. Men came down with parachutes, one not too far from us.

The planes flew on past, and then the bombs were dropped on Berlin. I'll never forget how the earth shook under us. We thought the end of the world had come. Our horses tore their harnesses from fear.

You know, when we were lying there, I noticed how the ground and grass smelled so fresh. Nature was beginning to come alive again; spring was coming! I thought how nice spring would be, if only we had peace. Here nature was coming to life, and only a few miles away, death. People were being burned by the phosphorous bombs or buried in the shattered homes. How can we ever understand the hatred of people, and the leaders of people, the governments? They were worse than wild animals who, after all, kill only when they are hungry.

After the bombing ended, two soldiers came and helped me put the horses and harnesses in order. What a horror when we got onto the street again. In front of us, Berlin was a sea of flames and smoke. The children were horrified like me. Buildings were smashed and burning. Even the tar on the street was burning.

When we got to Elise, we were so happy to see each other. But we didn't want to stay there long. That night there was another raid, and we had to stay in the air raid bunker. There we sat, with only a few candles for light. After they burned down, it was pitch dark. We sat all in a row, Erna the oldest, then Hilma, and then me with little Gerda on my lap.

I don't know how long it lasted until the all clear sounded. Then Erna — she was seven at the time — said, "The man next to me is very cold." He was dead, from a heart attack or something. It took Erna a long time to stop always thinking about it — she still talks about it today. That was the raid at Teltow, Berlin.

You know, during those dangerous times families stayed together as much as possible — like during the air raids. If something should happen to one, it would happen to all. Or all would be spared.

We packed Elise's stuff together — the little she had — and went immediately back to Züllichendorf where we were twenty-five miles away from Berlin — and a lot safer.

Major bombing raids were a new experience for the Weisses since they had not lived near a large city and they had also been in eastern Germany which was mostly out of range of the British and American bomber squadrons. But their Berlin raid was not untypical for most other Germans, at least in the last year of the war, when Allied fighters were able to escort the bombers to most places in western and central Germany. At this time, Berlin was being bombed almost every day. And, on February 13-14, just seventy-five miles south of the Weisses, the most devastating air raid of the war took place at Dresden. The city was crowded with refugees fleeing the Red Army as the Weisses had, and the raid by both American and British bombers killed unknown numbers — some estimates say 135,000 people.

So my sister-in-law Elise lived with us. She had no children, and her husband had been drafted into the *Volkssturm* (People's Army) at the end of January 1945. No one knew where he was. Later we learned he had been captured and sent to Russia along with seven other men originally from our hometown. Some years later — in the 1950s, one returned from the Russian POW camps.

"The other seven won't come back — I was together with them, but they're all dead. They were starved to death. They fed us so little that the body just wasted away, and people got sick and died. I'm the only one left to tell you."

The Americans and the Russians Arrive

In the middle of April, unexpectedly and without fighting, this other army with a different language appeared. In the beginning we didn't know who they were. That they weren't Russian, we knew, because we were familiar with the Russian language. Everybody said they were Americans. They had advanced without having to fight, because the Germans wanted the American and the English troops to occupy all of Germany, instead of the Russians. We didn't know Germany was already divided up differently. So the American troops stayed in Luckenwalde only two weeks.

After the Americans withdrew, the Russians came with tanks. By the first night, a family was shot. Young women and girls were raped. People tried to stay inside as much as possible, to keep away from the Russians. You never knew what could happen. Many other people just fled to the West. They disappeared overnight, leaving everything behind.

The first thing the Russians did was to look for watches, then they raped the women. They came looking for the daughter of the lady where we lived. Well, I was pregnant with our fourth child — to be born in another month or two, and the daughter, she was lucky, too. There was a prisoner of war, a short, dark, Serbian fellow, and she lived with him. So when the Russians came, he hid her under the straw by the cows. Whenever Russian soldiers came looking for women, he went to feed the cows. That way he would be there, if they found her.

He was a nice man. Gerda had pneumonia then, and he used to carry her around. A good friend of his, a doctor, told me to put a damp towel on her back, and make sure she would always be moving. "If she gets past eight or nine days, she'll get over it," he said. And she did.

So Immanuel's immediate family, as well as many of his relatives, survived the war:

Both my brothers were older than I, and they survived the war, too. Willy was eleven years older, a city clerk in the mayor's office in Bessarabia. He worked for the government in Stiermark, Austria, and didn't have to do any fighting.

My other brother, Theophil, was resettled in Warthegau as a farmer, like me. He was eighteen years older than I. In 1945, when he was forty-seven, he was drafted into the *Volkssturm* (militia) to stop the Russians. After the Russians captured him, he was taken to a barn along with thirty or forty others. One by one they took the prisoners away and shot them. After taking about a dozen, they stopped—before they got to him.

My three sisters weren't so lucky with their husbands. One was killed in the war on the Eastern Front, one starved to death in a Russian prison camp, and one came back a cripple. Johanna lost her only brother in the war, too.

Obviously the men paid the greatest cost of the Nazi aggression. Records show that of the 351 men and boys from Immanuel's Bessarabian village who had to fight in a war not of their making, 174 survived and 177 didn't.

But women had to pay, too. Many were not so fortunate as Johanna and her girls in surviving and also in avoiding a "fate worse than death." The Germans have collected volumes of depositions—many fully verified, of what happened to civilians at the end of the war—stories, for example, of women forced into brothels or being raped regularly for months after the war by strangers breaking into their shelters.

Some German civilians survived because of acts of kindness on the part of their "enemies." One deposition tells how a farmer's wife watched Russian troops pull her husband down from their wagon and shoot him. But the Polish women in the wagon—the family's workers, threw their shawls over her out of loyalty and pity, and successfully hid her.

The general feeling at the time, however, was that the Germans were collectively guilty of the brutalities committed by the Nazis. President Roosevelt wrote Secretary of War Stimson in 1944, "The German people as a whole must have it driven home to them that the whole nation has engaged in a lawless conspiracy against the decencies of modern civilization" (de Zayas, 14).

The Czechs, for example, after suffering terribly under a brutal Nazi occupation, got revenge by taking over the Nazi concentration camp at Theresienstadt and replacing the Jews with ethnic Germans. One of the Jews reported:

> Many among them (the ethnic Germans) had undoubtedly become guilty during the years of occupation, but in the majority they were children and juveniles, who had only been locked up because they were Germans... The people were abominably fed and mistreated, and they were no better off than one was used to from German concentration camps.... (Schieder, 76).

The total number of German civilians living in the annexed eastern third of Germany, plus those in other Eastern European countries living as minorities, was sixteen million. Approximately two million of them were killed, either at the end of the war or in the months afterward as the people of Eastern Europe exacted revenge on those who had not succeeded in fleeing.

Chapter 7

Prying the Family Loose from the Communists

Masses of people moved across Germany in the months right after the war's end. Some ten million Germans had fled from the bombing of the cities and were living in rural villages. They would now return to learn if family or friends were alive and if their homes still existed. Germans who had remained in the cities travelled in the opposite direction, seeking food in the rural areas.

Other Germans travelled between occupation zones. Some two million felt uncomfortable enough about the Russians to give up their homes and cross into the western zones of occupation. A half million went in the opposite direction during the year and a half immediately after the end of the war.

Some ten million forced laborers and several million concentration camp inmates survived the war and were now free to go to their various homes. Foreign workers living in the Soviet Zone were sent home whether or not they wanted to leave. In the Western Zones, only people from Russia were forcibly repatriated, keeping the promise made to Stalin at Yalta.

Stalin considered any of his people in the West as tainted. Altogether this was a large number: two million Soviets were German POWs and survived captivity; two million Soviet forced laborers were liberated by the Allies; and perhaps another million refugees — such as Ukrainians, Cossacks, Latvians, Lithuanians, Estonians, and others who had lived in the German-occupied Soviet Union — had fled together with the retreating Germans because they hated Russians or communism, or both.

Perhaps a million of all these various people had actively supported the Germans against the Russians, in many cases because they had been forced to do so. For Stalin, these details did

81

not matter. There was no distinction between citizens who had remained loyal while in captivity and those who had collaborated. All were considered traitors. When his only son was captured by the Germans, Stalin refused the prisoner exchange offered by Hitler. To surrender instead of dying while fighting was dereliction of duty. The Soviet Union did not recognize the Geneva Convention, nor did they send Red Cross supplies to their captured soldiers. In fact, they even had some camps holding their POWs bombed by the Red Air Force.

The Western Allies had to use force to repatriate the two million Soviet POWs, forced laborers, and displaced persons within their own occupation zones. Some were shot immediately after they were handed over, and many of the others were sent to the Gulag. Apparently only 15 or 20 percent would go completely unpunished. So Immanuel had some cause to worry. Would the authorities — and especially the Soviets — learn that he was born in a Bessarabia that, in 1916, was still Russian and that he had fought against them in the German Army?

Searching

For five months, I worked on the farm at Wätzum, near Hildesheim. I got 18 *Reichsmarks* ($4.50 dollars) per week, plus my keep. But all the while, I was searching for my family. People all over Germany were looking for their families.

Every day some people from Bessarabia would walk through the village. One day a friend who worked in a nearby village — he was a refugee from the Banat — sent his daughter to tell me that another family with the same name as mine was travelling through. But they were no relation.

I went into the big cities — Hildesheim and Hanover — and checked the Red Cross lists of refugees for relatives or friends. Many times I found the right family name and sometimes even the right forename. But the rest of the information didn't check out — birthdate, birthplace, hometown.

Then in September, I travelled to Lüneburg. I rode on top of a railroad coal car, the only way a refugee ex-soldier without money could travel. There at the refugee center run by the Red Cross, I saw a fence with a whole lot of slips of paper pasted up—giving names and addresses. There was a sign on top, "WER SUCHT WEN," (who looks for whom). So I put my little paper up there, too.

The son of a neighbor from my hometown in Bessarabia happened to see my slip of paper while passing through Lüneburg after being released from a POW camp. So when he got to his parents in Luckenwalde, they then passed on the word to Johanna that I was still alive.

I also tried to contact Johanna a second way. When I had to be hospitalized for a rupture operation, a soldier came through and visited a friend I made on the ward. I gathered from their conversation that he was traveling into the East Zone. So I asked him to carry along a letter for me. There had been no regular mail service to the East Zone since May.

The letter was addressed to a woman at her former address in Berlin. From the summer of 1943 onward, she and her four children had been evacuated from the bombing to live with us on the farm. Well, the letter eventually got to her, and she knew where Johanna and the children were. She was able to send it on. That way Johanna found out where I was, although I was still in the dark about them.

It wasn't till the mail began again, after October 24, 1945, that I found out all were safe—Johanna, the three girls, and a new baby boy born four months earlier!

Then I got a visit from my brother-in-law, Reinhold, but he told me it was better not to try to go into the East Zone—too dangerous! The Russians might imprison me because I was Russian-born and had fought against them.

Into the Russian Zone

But come what may, I was going to get my family out. So I left for the Russian Zone with Reinhold and another Bessarabian, after first getting a *Zuzugsgenehmigung* (a permit) from the *Burgomeister* allowing my family to live in my village.

There we were, standing in front of the barrier on the East Zone border, thousands of people on the west side who wanted to go east. Across the way were thousands who wanted to go west. At 10 a.m. they lifted the gate and let us go across first, one by one. We went first because there were always fewer going over to the Russians than those trying to leave the Russians. The Russians counted us going over to them, and then at noon they would let the same number — and no more, cross to the west. The rest of the people on the other side had to wait another day, till more people showed up to go into the Russian Zone.

After we passed through the gate, we had to be registered in a barracks. My heart was beating, because I didn't have an *Ausweis* (an identity card). All I had was a paper showing I was released from the English POW camp. But I got through okay.

Everybody ran quickly to the train station to get a place on a train. But there was a mass of people already waiting. Finally we saw some smoke — a train was coming. But it was just a locomotive and two passenger cars — for thousands of people!

But this little train stopped right in front of us. Everyone stormed through the doors and windows of the two cars. Every place was crammed full. People stood between the cars and sat on the roof, they even hung from the sides.

We had to change trains a few times, too, and then walk seven more miles, but we finally got to Züllichendorf, the village where our families were. What a joy to see each other again. It was by God's grace.

We immediately made plans to travel to the West. No one could be sure the border would be open another day. Besides my wife and children, I found my three sisters. Two had lost their husbands in the war, and the third — her husband was back, but missing one of his eyes and one of his arms.

Escape By Boxcar

So we all got ready; it didn't take long because there wasn't much to pack. We went to the railroad and rented an empty boxcar for the ride to the border. Then we sat and waited. We were twenty–five or thirty people, two–thirds children.

Finally the train left. We went through Luckenwalde to Halle, where the train stopped. There trains from different directions came together, and there were other refugees like us at the station — ten boxcars of refugees altogether. All wanting to go to the West.

After twenty-four hours of waiting and after some of the women went to see the Russian commissar, a locomotive came and hooked up. But it pulled us to the east! We thought, "Now they're shipping us to Siberia!" After a long time, the train stopped at another station, and police stood guard at the doors, letting no one out.

We told them we needed some food for the children and milk for the babies. Our Erich was six months then and always got his milk warmed with a candle. So the police said, "Okay." There were facilities from an earlier German canteen, where two religious sisters prepared warm food for refugees. They got a one-pot meal ready for our group. But before they could serve it, the locomotive started up again, pulling us farther to the east!

There we sat in the unheated boxcar, hungry and feeling pretty defeated, each of us busy with his or her own thoughts about what the future held. The children were tired and hungry. Yet they didn't cry; they had an understanding beyond their years even though they were anxious about what would happen next.

Two hours later, about 10 p.m., we arrived back in Luckenwalde! It had taken us three days of travel to get back to where we started. Of course it wasn't far; trains in those days travelled slowly and stopped at every little station. But at least we got back to Luckenwalde, instead of ending up farther east somewhere.

This time we didn't see any police when we looked out. So each person slung their bundle over their back, and the mothers took the children in hand. Into the fields we went, and got away.

That very night, my brother-in-law and I went into Berlin and over to the British Sector. We signed up for a transport to West Germany. They saw we had a *Zuzugsgenehmigung* (a residence permit) for the British Zone of Occupation. Only they couldn't take us right away. Could we wait a month or two?

Russians and More Russians

I went up to Berlin and the British Sector two more times to see whether we'd gotten on the transport list yet. We couldn't write and ask. It had to be done in person. Otherwise people in Luckenwalde would find out we wanted to escape from the Russian Zone.

The way from Züllichendorf to Luckenwalde was seven miles, and there was a Russian military camp in between. We had to go past there often, and each time I was anxious that they might stop and interrogate me or ask for an *Ausweis* (identity card). But it went all right. One time on the way home, the Russians even gave us a ride on a wagon. We got off before they went into the camp!

Another time there was trouble on the train coming back from Berlin. German civilians always had to travel in third class cars, Russian military used the second or first class cars. Each time the train started up, Russian soldiers came back into our packed third class cars and pawed the women and grabbed their pocketbooks. Finally, someone pulled the emergency brake, and the train stopped right in the middle of nowhere. The Soviets just jumped out and ran back into their own cars, so people couldn't point them out to the officers.

One time Johanna came along with me to sell my sister's team of horses to the farmer who was keeping them. The train on the way back was the last of the day and it was full in third class. But the second class car for the Russian military was almost empty, so we went in there, and stood in the corridor. Then two Russians in uniform came and took Johanna, with me following, back into their compartment. They asked us all kinds of questions—including whether Hitler still lived, and where he might be. We were really anxious. Why were they asking us all these questions? At the next station, the two soldiers went out and brought two women back, and began again with the questions. Finally, at Luckenwalde, we were able to leave.

Right after Christmas, I went into Berlin again. The British said our transport would leave on the third of January. We should all be ready the day before—in the British Sector of Berlin. So on the second, we hired a driver and an old army truck. We were also taking along my sister with her two children, eight and twelve years old, and Johanna's sister-in-law with her three children ranging from three to eight years old. After they lost their husbands in the war, I couldn't leave them alone in the Russian Zone—even though we didn't have any *Zuzugsgenehmigung* (residence permits) for them.

We paid the driver well and told him we had to get into the British Sector of Berlin. The way we did it, we all sat in the back of the truck, behind the cab, and the driver then put a canvas cover over the top of us so no one could see us underneath. It worked!

Next was the problem of getting onto the transport from Berlin to the British Zone of Occupation. My *Zuzugsgenehmigung* was good for six persons—Johanna, our four children, and me—not for thirteen people. When the secretary checked us for the transport and asked for my permit, I showed it to her, but pulled it away real quickly.

"How many people?"

I told her, "Thirteen." Not the "six" actually on the permit.

The same thing happened after we went across the Russian Zone and got ready to go into the British Zone. Neither the Russian or the British soldier saw that we were thirteen instead of six.

But we had one more test. As our train stood ready to go into the British Zone, some Russian soldiers came along and knocked on the door to our boxcar—we were in boxcars used to transport cattle or grain. The Russians were coming down the line of boxcars, one by one, robbing the luggage people had with them.

The Russian soldiers called out, "*Otkreu dwer,*" or "open the door." We asked who they were.

"Open, or we'll break it down."

We opened. A Russian soldier came in and asked where we were going.

"Home."

He gave us a really evil look and got ready to throw our bags out. We could see the other soldiers standing outside the cars ahead of us, going through luggage.

Just at this point, the officials finished with the border-check. The train started to move—westward! So the Russian had to jump out quickly without taking anything. We were lucky because our boxcar was next to the last. The Russians just ran out of time. That's how we made it to the West and freedom!

87

Chapter 8

Refugee Life In Germany

The Germans refer to the period at the war's end as "Time Zero." The devastation and economic collapse were worse than at any other time in German history. If people could overcome their grief over those killed in the war, they still had to face almost insurmountable practical problems.

Homeless refugees numbering perhaps 6 million – mostly women, children, and elderly men – crowded into the occupation zones of the Western Allies alone. They came from Prussia, Pomerania, Silesia and other territories annexed by Poland and the Soviet Union, and from the ethnic German enclaves in Poland, Czechoslovakia, Hungary, Romania, Yugoslavia, and Russia. The number of those expelled and taking refuge in West Germany would eventually reach 10 million. In addition there were untold numbers of Poles, Balts, Ukrainians, and others who wanted to stay in the Western occupation zones; they did not want to return to their former homes.

Shelter was scarce even for those whose homes were in the territory left to Germany; a majority of the cities had experienced over 50 percent destruction. Of the 16,000,000 houses in the four zones of occupation, 2,340,000 were totally destroyed, and another 4,000,000 had at least 25 percent damage. City people were lucky to live in a cellar or basement underneath a ruined building. In West Germany, some 20,000,000 were homeless. In the British Zone, the northwestern, industrialized part of Germany where Immanuel's family found themselves, the average dwelling space for an entire family was 9 by 6 feet.

Everything else was scarce. The Ruhr could produce only about one quarter of its former output of coal. Food was in specially short supply because the main agricultural regions of Germany were in the East, in the territories detached by Poland as compensation for their own land annexed by Russia, plus in the Russian Zone of

Occupation. In the British Zone, food rations were set at 1,550 calories, about half the normal consumption in a Western European country.

But matters worsened. The Soviets had agreed, at the Potsdam meetings of August 1945, that they would ship food from the agricultural territories they occupied in exchange for industrial equipment plus industrial production from the British and American Zones. This was in addition to the industrial equipment the Soviets were already stripping from their own zone as reparations. But the promised food shipments were not made by the Soviets. The British eventually had to reduce German rations to 1,015 calories per day. Matters worsened as the millions of expelled Germans from the East arrived in the Western zones of occupation. Even two years after the war's end, in April 1947, people in West Germany averaged only 1,040 calories per day, compared to the 4,200 calories a soldier in the American occupation forces got.

When the British and Americans saw that no food was being sent from the Soviet Zone, they stopped their industrial shipments to the East. It became clear that Stalin wanted to honor only the parts of the Potsdam agreements that suited him. Relations between the Soviets and the Western Allies were quickly cooling and moving toward the Cold War. A couple of years later, the Soviets would take active measures such as cutting off all food and electricity and shutting off access routes to the sectors of Berlin they had agreed the Western Allies could occupy. But Immanuel and his family headed to a more familiar environment, to the small peasant village.

In the devastation and chaos and grief that was Germany, Immanuel and Johanna's Swabian work ethic and frugality would stand them in good stead. Coming as they did from generations of independent peasants, they saw their salvation on the land, working hard and saving their earnings. The national motto of the Swabians is, "Work, work, and build a house."

Instead of going back to the farm, we went to Lauenstein, also near Hildesheim, where there was a furniture factory and better pay. But they didn't give me a job, so I had to go back to doing farm work on a big estate and for a miserable wage. We lived in two small, dark rooms.

It was January and all of us—Johanna and the children as well as I—had to go into the woods to get firewood. There was no alternative, no coal to buy, nothing else available. So we collected wood. We had no saw or axe, and couldn't buy any. Cutting trees wasn't permitted anyway. We just gathered fallen wood. There wasn't much after seven years of war. The forest was very, very clean, but we were happy just to gather small branches and cut them up with a borrowed hatchet. Otherwise we wouldn't have survived.

Return to Swabia

I thought, if only we could get to some other country like America. It wouldn't matter that all we owned was the clothes on our backs. We would have opportunity. In Germany there was no opportunity for us. But other countries wouldn't take Germans.

My brother was in South Germany, in *Schwabenland* (Swabia). He wrote that he had found us a place. So we travelled back to the land where our ancestors had lived before they went to Bessarabia 150 years earlier.

When we arrived in the village of Prevorst, we again found dark rooms waiting for us—two completely empty rooms, no chairs to sit on, not even a light bulb. What an arrival. Night came and we were finally able to get a light bulb. But we hadn't a thing to eat and nothing to sleep on.

Then there was a knock on the door. It was three children—Gertrut, Erika, and Erich—who lived across the street. Their father had a blacksmith shop and was also a farmer. One girl had a big round loaf of *Bauernbrot* (peasant bread) in her arms, the other a little basket full of apples and a can of meat. What a blessing in our time of need. The boy had a pillow for our Erich, who was just eight months old then. We cried tears of joy.

We felt better; these gifts gave us some hope that people here had their hearts in the right place, that they had compassion. The people in Prevorst were just small farmers—the largest farm was only twelve acres. They had to work hard to survive. But almost without exception, they were good to us.

So we ate our bread and apples. But not the meat, because we didn't have a can opener. Besides, we figured we'd save it for later. Who knew where our next meal would come from? Then someone called out that we should go down to the *Krone* (the inn) where they had guest rooms. So we slept there, quite well. They even made breakfast for us. The next day we went back to our rooms, and people gave us furniture. From this person came a bench or a chair and from that person a table or a bed. It soon was livable.

Gradually we became known to the people, and we got work. The next day, I chopped firewood for a man and got a meal plus some food for my family. I also started work for the people at the inn. The pay was RM30 ($7.50) per week. Sundays I was also paid a *Bauernbrot* (farmhouse bread) and a couple pounds of meat or canned wurst.

To be paid in food was really important because food was hard to get. You could buy food only up to the limit of the rationing stamps issued by the government, and that wasn't much. Starting in July 1946, we were permitted about two pounds of bread, seven ounces of meat, and about five ounces of butter. That was a week's worth of food for one person. It was a lot of bread, but not much to put on it. Sometimes I might eat a whole pound of bread in a sitting—bread with nothing on it. Other meals were just potatoes—potatoes without meat and without gravy. Just plain boiled potatoes. From time to time, we did get special ration stamps to buy things like herring, eggs, or wine. But the food ration stamps didn't let you buy enough to live on. You had to get extra food some other way. That's where the ration of three cigarettes per day—for adults—helped. We would trade them for food or clothes. They were worth as much as RM5 ($1.25) per cigarette.

Everything—I mean, everything—was rationed in Germany after the war, not just food. Clothes were rationed, pots and pans, dishes, glasses, spoons, forks—everything. Building materials were rationed—wood, cement, hammers, saws, even nails. There were millions of refugees and most of the factories were destroyed. That's why everything had to be rationed.

So we worked a lot of times just for food. Sometimes Johanna and I and the older girls—they were eight and five—helped one of the small farmers with the haying, and we were paid with a meal or a loaf of *Bauernbrot*. Johanna and the children also went gleaning after the harvest. They might get twenty-five pounds of grain in a day. At home they'd pound the heads, clean out the chaff, and then take it to the mill to be ground into flour. They also helped to harvest potatoes and got paid with potatoes. That's how we were able to eat all those potato meals.

It sounds crazy that we would work for just a meal, but we were so hungry we were happy to do it. And at a meal the farmers let us eat as much as we wanted. The food was worth more than money during that time.

The farmers always had plenty of butter, meat, and bread, and they used that food to trade for clothing, building materials, or whatever. They made good use of the black market. But refugees like us could trade only our labor. Many times we had no other way to get some bread or meat than to barter our work; we had no things to trade on the black market. That made us start to think maybe we should leave the country, go somewhere else. We didn't want to live on handouts, be beggars. And during much of that time, up to 1950 or so, we couldn't be sure that Germany would become a stable, law-abiding place to live.

On the other hand, my nephews and nieces would ask me, "*Onkel* (Uncle), how can you go to another country with five children and without money or knowing the language?" See, we had another baby, Siegfried, in 1951. But I always gave them the same answer, "With God's help, with a spirit of enterprise, with the luck of good health, and by setting a goal for yourself, that's how you can achieve an awful lot."

But it was hard. When someone is so poor, like we were, and sees little children needing everyday things like food, and it's not possible to buy it for them...and the children's eyes are so sad and so innocent... only people who have seen it firsthand can understand it. To leave and immigrate to America was for both Johanna and me such a clear choice. We knew we could make it if we stayed healthy. That gave us the strength to withstand everything. We had only to look forward. To work and to save!

The main blessing in our life then was that after all the years of war we lived in peace. We could sleep at night. No planes bombing or strafing people in the streets or fields. The family was together, too, no longer having to think maybe we wouldn't live to see each other again. So we weren't worried about not having things.

What was also good was that my brothers and sisters and also Johanna's family were nearby. We were able to share our burdens. It didn't change things, but we felt better being able to talk about it with others.

We also appreciated being in *Schwabenland*, rather than in North Germany. We could speak the dialect, and the people could understand us, too. We felt more comfortable with the people — they were like us.

Saved by Beechnuts and Moles

The fantastic beechnut harvest of 1947 helped us survive those years when oil and fat were rationed and so hard to get. Inside the shells of these nuts were three little kernels, each about as big as a corn kernel.

Because I was a part-time woodcutter in the forests, I knew where to find the big beech trees. We would take a twig broom and sweep up the fallen nuts, and then dump them onto a blanket. We'd shake the nuts and leaves and everything up in the air, maybe five or six feet up, and the wind would clean it out, leaving mostly nuts. Sometimes we also climbed up to shake the nuts down onto the blankets.

Eight pounds of these kernels could be made into one liter of oil at the mill. We used to go out everyday after work, as well as Saturdays and Sundays. We collected over five hundred pounds by winter. The sixty-five to seventy liters of oil lasted us almost two years. We used it very sparingly at home. We also traded a lot for flour and, especially, for clothing and shoes, which we couldn't get for money or from farm work. The oil made a real difference.

Besides the farm work, I worked winters as a tree-feller for the state, at seventy-five *Pfennige* (eighteen cents) per hour. That's where I was able to get the wood for our cooking and heating.

I had another part-time job for the state: I trapped voles, big mice four or five inches long, and also moles. These would make burrows and chew the roots of fruit trees. I made more money at that job than any other job I had — because it was piece work. Besides the RM20 ($5) a week the government paid me, I got a bounty of 25 *Pfennige* (6 cents) per mole and 50 *Pfennige* (12 cents) per mouse. And I could sell the moleskins for 25 *Pfennige* more. The other good thing about the job—I was on my own. I learned how to set two traps in each burrow, so I got them either way they went. I'd put a stick with a number on it by each trap to make sure I checked on each one. Each day I laid a hundred traps over twenty acres of orchard, and the next morning I'd pick them up and set them somewhere else.

The season was eight weeks in the spring and twelve weeks in the fall, and I worked in a dozen different villages. I'd go around looking for fresh mounds of dirt, and I'd set the traps there. After setting my routine traps in the morning, I set extra traps in the afternoon for farmers who were having special trouble, and they'd give me food, like canned sausage, or maybe a little money. Sometimes I trapped as many as thirty-five or forty a day. I could make almost double my wages. I did this from 1946 until 1948, when the government stopped the trapping program. After that, I was able to get a full-time job cutting trees—for the Löwenstein forest district.

In 1947 I also started raising domestic mice for a company. I bought a breeding pair for RM7.50 and was paid RM1.50 for each eight-week-old mouse I raised. They used them for research. At the end, I had ten breeding pairs. I made good money. But other people got into the business, too, and after a year I had to give it up.

I was always looking for some kind of work. At the time, there was no welfare available. All of Germany was in need of welfare! This made us—and Germany—tough. People used to say, "You could be Jesus Christ, it doesn't matter. You still have to help yourself."

Slowly we moved ahead. We bought ten baby chicks and raised them so we would get up to eight or nine eggs in a day. What wealth! Next, we bought a young pig, and eventually we had meat. To get feed for the chickens and the pig, I worked for a farmer, and I got all their kitchen garbage. For the pig, the children also used to collect grass and weeds by hand, from along the road sides.

We saved to buy an old bike so I could ride to work. Next, we bought an old, but still good bedroom set. Slowly, one by one, we got things—a cooking pot, a chair, and so on. In 1947 we were able to buy a used radio, what progress!

So after a while we could again at least start to think about the future. But wherever we looked, it was as if there were a wall around us. If you wanted to move to the city to get a better job, you couldn't get housing. If you wanted to start some kind of business, banks wouldn't loan money — unless you were already established. And Prevorst was too much of a backwater to consider starting a business anyway.

Then there were the living conditions in Prevorst. We lived so close. Three different families shared the same kitchen. We all came from the same hometown; we were all friends, but still... And Johanna and I and the five children lived in just two rooms.

All this was over and above the constant struggle to get enough food for the family, especially for the growing children. It was so bad that our oldest daughter, Erna, even had to be sent for a while to a state convalescent home in the Black Forest. There she got good food — rich foods like butter, and she was able to come home after five weeks. During those times, even in 1947, many German children were malnourished.

Three years after the war, in 1948, the German economy was still in shambles. A major stumbling block was the Reichsmark *currency, wildly inflated from Hitler's deficit spending during the 1930s and during the war. There were plenty of* Reichsmarks *but little to buy.*

American cigarettes were the real currency — on the illegal black market. People withheld goods from government controlled channels to sell them illegally for cigarettes. Germans used the Reichsmark *only where they were forced to, such as buying and selling rationed goods. On the black market,* Reichsmarks *were almost worthless. A worker might get a wage of one* Reichsmark *per hour, but found the money useful mainly for the limited goods the government controlled as part of the rationing system. On the black market, it took three* Reichsmarks, *or three hours of labor, to buy just one American cigarette.*

The German economy was thus hampered by an inflexible rationing system meant to deal with a huge overhang of worthless currency and by a diversion of people's energies to speculate in an illegal market based on American cigarettes. Then, in a bold stroke, the West German government issued a new currency and eliminated most rationing. The Germans trusted the new money and applied themselves to honest work instead of the black market. German industrial production would soar by 50 percent in the next six months!

Our Savings Are Lost

On Sunday, June 20, 1948, we heard on the radio, "From today, we have new money, the *Deutschmark* (DM)." It was the *Währungsreform* (currency reform). Everyone had to give up the old *Reichsmarks*; they weren't worth anything. So there our saved-up money was gone!

Everyone could change sixty of the old into sixty of the new money. That's all. Any money you had over sixty *Reichsmarks* ($15 dollars) was worthless. For us, that was about RM3,900 in cash we'd saved. While we were in Warthegau, Johanna saved some money from the milk, from sugar beets, and so on. And I sent her the three *Reichsmarks* per day I was paid as a soldier. She took this money when she fled the Russians. After that, she also got about RM200 per month government support as a refugee family with children. There wasn't much to spend money on during the war or after the war, so she saved most all of it, only to lose it in 1948.

But there was more. We had RM7,000 in our checking account in Warthegau, and those *Reichsmarks* were kaput, too. Maybe the government thought that the money could have been taken out before we fled. In any event, our checking account from Warthegau was worth nothing. A savings account of RM 3,000 from Warthegau turned out to be almost worthless, too. Years later we got maybe 10 percent of it; I can't remember exactly. Except for that small fraction, we lost all our savings in life up to then.

I should say that the German government eventually gave us some money for the property we had to leave when the Soviets took over Bessarabia. Our farm — the eighty acres, the animals, the machinery, the crops growing and in storage, as well as the house and household things — was all valued at RM52,700 in September of 1940. We were supposed to be reimbursed in Germany, and I suppose on that basis they put us on the farm in

Warthegau — where we also got paid in hatred and envy from the Polish people.

The Soviet government was supposed to reimburse Germany after they took our property in Bessarabia. I recall hearing that the Soviets wanted to pay in grain, but I don't think they did. They should have been able to, because they have very good grain lands in the Soviet Union, and wherever Germans had settled, like in Bessarabia, there was a surplus of grain and animals. That the Soviet Union would ever have to import grain from the U.S. and elsewhere, like today, we would have never believed. I still can't believe it — but of course, the communist system just doesn't work anywhere.

In any event, sometime towards the end of the 1950s, when Germany again had its own government, a law was passed to compensate refugees from the East and bombed-out people for their lost property. That's how we got some money for our Bessarabian farm. Everybody who owned property in Germany at that time had to pay extra taxes for many years so those who lost property through the war could be compensated. It was called the "Equalization of Burdens Law."

When we were eventually reimbursed, we got only a small fraction of what we should have, with no interest. But at least we got something. We have to respect Germany. Most countries would repudiate whatever debts they could. We give thanks for the German sense of obligation and justice.

Of course, back in 1948 we didn't know we'd get a partial reimbursement for our lost farm in another fifteen years or so. We just knew we lost our lifetime savings — all we had left after losing our farms and possessions in the East and in Bessarabia.

But the currency reform really improved the economy in Germany. It did away with most of the rationing, and the black market was wiped out. Now you could buy many things that you never even saw in a store before. People were willing to sell because they got money worth something. Our income didn't allow us to buy anything other than the most necessary things. But we could see, if you worked hard, then it would eventually be possible to buy things. They were available, if you had the money. Before it didn't make as much sense for people to work hard, just for worthless pieces of paper. Before, people were just interested in getting cigarettes!

In 1948, I gave up my woodcutter job and worked in a factory started by a Bessarabian from my hometown. I made cement blocks and roof tiles. The work was hard, and the travel made it harder. I left home at 5 a.m. and walked two miles through the woods to catch a bus to the city of Heilbronn. I worked there six months, but then fell sick. After I got out of the hospital, I found a new job working for the police. I helped take fingerprints for the *Personalausweis* (the new personal identity card). But I really didn't want to stay there. I'd had enough to do with uniforms and guns in my life.

A Better Job, But Still a Refugee

In July of 1949, I got a job as a laborer on a road-gang, working for the state. I was a street-worker, second class, working on both repairs and rebuilding.

Summers we did the rebuilding work. We'd use pick and shovel to dig out six to eight inches, and then we'd set big stones in there, flat side down, with smaller ones piled on top. Then they were smashed down with a ten- or fifteen-pound hammer. Next, the scraper and steam roller went over in turns, putting fine gravel on top, and finally lime and water, all rolled smooth and hard. It took forever to build a road this way with so much handwork. But everybody wanted a job, and this made for plenty of jobs.

In the spring of 1950, the *Strassenwart* (the man in charge...) of our stretch of road, nominated me to become a *Strassenwart*, too. This was a salaried job, and it included allowances for each child, twenty *Deutschmark* ($5) each. So I went to Heilbronn and passed the *Strassenwart* exam with a *"sehr gut"* (very good). I was put in charge of repairs for a stretch of road around Obergruppenbach and Wüstenhausen.

A section of my road had to be completely rebuilt, so I also got to learn most of the different work involved in rebuilding. Then, in 1951, the *Strassenwart* in charge of the rebuilding ran into trouble. His boss, the *Strassenmeister*, came on an inspection and found out he was doing lousy work. The next day the head people in the department came. I happened to be busy there with the steam roller. They called me over and put me in full charge of the twelve or fourteen men working at the site. I told them I was younger than any other *Strassenwart* and I had less experience. The older ones might not take orders or advice from me. They told me not to worry, I would have full authority. Then the bosses left! But I had no problems. The street rebuilding was completed under my charge.

Now, the road I was responsible for, Auenstein to Untergruppenbach, was only about ten miles away from Prevorst, but the bus connections were very poor. I tried to get a house nearby, in a new development of ten new houses being built. A house was promised and I was supposed to move in. But a local man opened the house up and just moved in overnight! And the housing officials and police couldn't—or maybe didn't want to—force him out.

So I had to keep on commuting from Prevorst, leaving my home at 5:45 a.m., working all day outside, whatever the weather, in cold or rain, then commuting home again and getting back at 6:30 p.m. I had to spend nearly thirteen hours away from home, but I was being paid for only eight hours. I told my superiors; I really needed a house nearby. They were able to arrange one in the next village, but there was no school there for my children. They would still have to walk to another village for school.

By then, I had been thinking of leaving Germany for a long time. We located a distant relative in Medicine Hat, Alberta, Canada. In the summer of 1948, he wrote that he'd bring us over the next year. But then we learned he lost all his crops from hail and he could no longer help us. I suppose he was also thinking about the problems of sponsoring a family with so many children. We were disappointed.

Things were gradually getting better in Germany. But I still had to remind my children, "When we get to America, we'll be able to eat meat—as much as we want. I'll be able to go hunting and shoot wild animals." That's what I kept telling them.

I couldn't really feel good in Germany. I felt too hemmed in. I wanted to have a place I could call my own; I wanted to have some land where I could plant things again. That was impossible in Germany. The people who had it made would shove us refugees away; we were not fully respected. That really upset me. I made up my mind that I wasn't going to be a stick-in-the-mud. I wanted to prove that I could make it, and I'd go to any country to do it, even Australia or America.

That's what gave me strength. I kept looking out for the opportunities that were bound to come knocking. In America, well, I knew that it wouldn't be simple. The language was different, and we had five young children. But it was tough getting enough food for your family wherever you lived, in Germany or America.

Chapter 9

Land of Opportunity

Immanuel and Johanna didn't know that many Bessarabians had earlier immigrated to America. The original nine thousand Germans answering the Tsar's invitation to Bessarabia between 1814 and 1842 eventually prospered and flourished. But almost all their children also wanted to be farmers, and the population outgrew the land available. In addition, the Russians withdrew special privileges granted by the Tsar, such as freedom from military service. Roughly 25,000 Bessarabian Germans left up to 1927, when Romania prohibited further emigration. Many of their descendants now live in North Dakota and across the border in Alberta, Canada.

But after World War II, immigration was not easy for the Bessarabian Germans. They were viewed as Germans and as such, enemies and undesirables. The only Germans allowed in were people with a special status – e.g., German Jews who had survived the Holocaust or American-born children of German descent who had been brought back to Germany by their parents in the 1920s or 1930s and had been trapped by the war.

With the passage of time and also with the advent of the Cold War with Russia, attitudes changed. In 1946, war brides, that is, German women who married American soldiers, were admitted. The Displaced Persons Acts of 1948 and 1950 opened the U.S. to people who could not return to their homes in communist–controlled countries, such as Latvia, Lithuania, and Estonia. Farmers were especially welcomed. Eventually, even ordinary Germans found they could again get visas under the quota system.

Sponsorship, however, was more difficult. An American had to guarantee housing and employment for the immigrant family.

In the summer of 1951 we heard that there were people in Stuttgart taking names for immigration to America through the Church World Service. The Lutherans, Catholics, Methodists — all the churches together — were financing it. So we put our names down. They took 54,000 names. It took a long time before they got all the information and background on us. In February 1952, Johanna's sister was called to report to a camp in Hanau. In March, it was our turn to go to the camp for ten days.

There they had all kinds of information about us — papers from Romania, from twenty years earlier. But I had no problem.

Getting a Sponsor

We passed all the political and health checks, but we had no sponsor in America. Then they told us, "The church will sponsor you, whatever your denomination." The Lutheran Church sponsored us, but only as far as New York City. There the local churches would find a sponsor.

We didn't know we actually had close relatives in the state of Washington who could have sponsored us. We only found that out in 1977 when we went to an American Historical Society of Germans from Russia convention in Lincoln, Nebraska. There were some nine hundred people in a church, watching a show with the various costumes people brought to the U.S. We didn't have a seat, so we stood in the back. Johanna saw a man, "He looks like a Weiss." Well, that wasn't his name, but his mother's. She was a second cousin to me!

Then we met my first cousin — our fathers had actually been brothers. He was only two years old when he left Bessarabia in 1898. First they went to Medicine Hat, Alberta, then to Yakima, Washington. They had it hard, no money, and they farmed in the old-fashioned way, like in Russia. Instead of a threshing machine, they'd find a level spot, water it, and let the horses pack it down hard as a stone. Then they'd put the grain there in loose piles and let the horses thresh it. But that's a whole other story...

The last thing we had to do at Hanau was get the approval of the American government officials. They brought up three things. First, would I fight for the U.S.?

"Yes." They made me sign a paper.

Then they said, "We want you to know you shouldn't plan on getting any help from the government."

"I'm coming to work."

Finally, they asked, "Do you want to change your name?" Some Germans changed their names for political reasons.

"No."

Going to America meant getting as far from the communists as I could. Many people in Germany were worried that things might explode again over there. I would have gone to Australia or South America if I couldn't have gotten into America.

You know, we could have wound up in Paraguay. After the war, the Bessarabian Germans wanted to emigrate somewhere as a group. Some sixty thousand got to West Germany — the rest of the original ninety thousand refugees were either dead or trapped in East Germany or Russian prison camps. Contacts were made with Paraguay, and a pastor, an agronomist, a teacher, and also a businessman, were sent to study the country. But they decided that the climate was so hot and humid that the school kids wouldn't be able to think straight. And where they wanted to settle us was rough forest with no roads or anything. Anyway, by then we weren't in West Germany anymore.

After our trip to Hanau, we had fourteen days to get everything ready to leave Germany. In that time, our house in Obergruppenbach was finally finished and ready for moving in. Forget it, we're going to America!

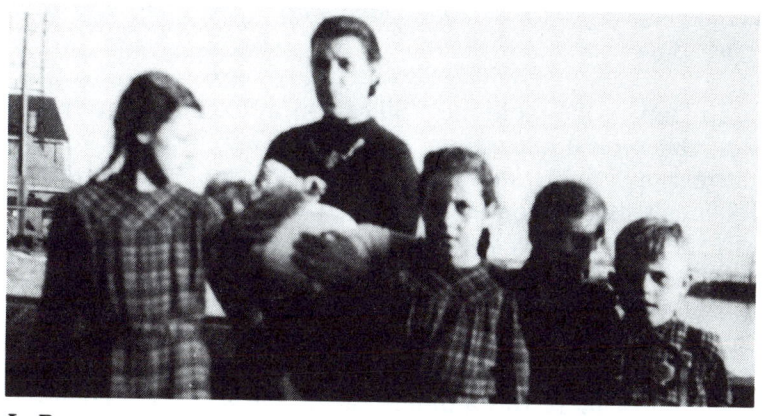

In Bremen, April 1952, Johanna and the five Weiss children await the ship that will carry them to a new life in the USA.

It was hard leaving Prevorst and all our relatives and friends from Bessarabia who lived in the area. It was especially hard on my brother's family because his kids were the same age as ours and they always played together. Willy told his family they would have to think of us as if we were dead because we just wouldn't see each other again. Of course, in just thirteen years, by 1965, it was easy to fly across the Atlantic, so we were able to see them in Germany. But they had changed in thirteen years, and we had changed in thirteen years, too.

So we took the train up to Bremen, and on the seventeenth of April, 1952, we left on *The General Harry Taylor* for "the land of unlimited possibilities."

On April 17, 1952, the Weiss family left Bremen on The General Harry Taylor *for New York along with 1,300 other German refugees.*

In Hanau, they told me, "Since you were in the cavalry in Romania, you'll make a good cowboy. There's a lady with a cattle ranch in Utah who will sponsor you." But I wrote Johanna's sister, who was already in America, to find a place for us. In New York City, we got a phone call that her sponsor would help us, too.

Before we left New York, we bought two loaves of bread to eat on the train. On the second day, the bread was almost gone, and we were starving — there were seven of us altogether. We didn't know there was a dining car on the train. We couldn't speak even a word of English to ask. When I made like I wanted to put something in my mouth and chew it, the conductor finally understood. But he just pointed off in one direction. We didn't know what he meant. In Germany we always just took sandwich makings. To eat out someplace would be too expensive. We finally figured there was no one who would understand German, so we didn't bother asking anymore.

In Chicago, we were met by two German-speaking women who took us by car to a restaurant. Then we waited at the station for our train connection and had another adventure. We saw people buying something orange-colored to drink. We never saw it before, and was it good! It was a Negro who served us. And the money was new to us, too. So we just put some coins on the table and let him take what he wanted. We were specially confused because the ten-cent piece was smaller than the five-cent piece, and neither had a number on it. We went by the size. We figured the bigger nickel must be worth more than the smaller dime.

Our sponsor in Iowa was a good man — he sponsored thirty-nine families! He owned a clothing store, and he was also a salesman for heavy equipment. His German parents had come to farm in Iowa, and he grew up speaking German. He went to a lot of trouble to help people, but with us he had a special problem in finding housing. No one wanted a family of seven. So he finally went to the local pastor.

Trapped by a Pastor

The pastor had room for us. He had only two children and a big house. We ate there, too. Johanna cooked for all, and she also watched the pastor's children so the wife could go out and work. On top of that, we paid the utilities. Naturally, they wouldn't like to see us leave.

But we were always hungry. I worked at a plasterboard factory where there was much heavy lifting and carrying, so I needed plenty of food for energy. But the pastor's wife told Johanna what food to cook. Our children were always hungry. For eleven people, there was just nothing on the table. See, the pastor didn't need much food. He didn't work hard and he slept in the morning. We had to send our older girls to a store for eggs and bread to eat later after dinner. The pastor's children ate eggs and bread with us, too.

107

So we told our sponsor, "We want out of the pastor's house," and he found us a place on a friend's farm nearby. The house was old but furnished with everything, even the towels. We thought it was so nice. The sponsor's friend told us, "I'll give you $100 a month, and I'll bring the pigs and chickens over. You raise them and we'll split the profit half-and-half."

"But I'm making more at the factory."

"If we get along, I'll raise your pay $25 in three months time and then again if we like you."

So we thought, we'll take it.

Then our sponsor phoned and asked, "Why didn't you take it?" Well, I think the pastor must have called the farmer to say we didn't want it.

Then there was another place; the pastor and his wife drove us there. It was a nice remodeled house together with farm buildings, right alongside a river. But the owner's wife asked me all kinds of suggestive questions, like whether there were many pretty women in Germany. Johanna was upset. Later, we learned what troubled them. The woman's brother had been in the army in Germany and had found a German girl there—leaving a wife and two children here. But they were still willing to have me to help on the farm and to do some construction work. We finally decided to take it. But by then, the pastor must have called it off again.

Then, we met a nice lady from Holland, and we told her how hard it was to find a place big enough for our family. She said she'd watch the newspaper for an apartment, and she found a house in town for only $60 a month. But I guess the pastor found out somehow. That deal fell through, too.

The pastor was really a good man—he helped our children study for Sunday School, and he was nice in other ways. But they did need us a lot, especially the wife. Three times they must have called it off. We don't want to think evil of them, but it sure wasn't nice for us. We wanted so badly to be on our own, to be independent. You know, maybe God wanted to test us somehow.

Then a lady in the pastor's church heard we were looking for a farm, and she told a relative who had lost his hired man. The farmer came one day and spoke to Johanna in German, and it sounded like a good arrangement. The pastor drove us out.

These people offered $150 a month, plus all the meat we wanted, two quarts of milk a day, two dozen eggs a week, and the house to live in. The house had only four small rooms, and we were seven in the family. But the man told us he'd build on, and so we made a deal. This deal we made between us, speaking in German, and the pastor or his wife couldn't do a thing! So a week later, on the Fourth of July, 1952, we moved in.

Farm Work Again

I worked hard there. At 5:30 in the morning, I started milking the cows and, except for some breakfast and lunch, I worked without stopping until 7 or 7:30 at night. I liked it; I was familiar with farm animals. We milked twenty cows and fed a hundred beef cattle and sixty pigs. I also knew planting and plowing from Bessarabia, but, of course, these things were done a little differently in America. Over there, we had no modern machines — hay balers, tractors, milking machines, and so on.

The hardest thing was learning English. And also the loneliness when we moved out of town to the farm. The children were used to playing with the neighboring children in Prevorst, and they had started to make friends here in town, too. But on the farm they were all alone. Sundays were the worst. In Germany, we used to walk over and visit my brother's family or other relatives in the next village. Here, Sunday was so empty, so meaningless.

After we bought a car in October, it was better. The car cost $650 — a lot of money, but we were no longer dependent on others. And everyone's English got better. We told the children, "Whoever learns English first will be our translator and go along with us in the car." So they all learned English pretty fast! And Johanna's sister and family came to live just three miles away, so Johanna wasn't so lonely anymore, either.

After a year, I told the boss I wanted more pay, $175 a month because I knew others got that much. He said, "No," but he did offer me a bonus in a year's time. I wanted money in hand, not promises. I even went back to the factory to try and get my old job back.

But then we found a man — he spoke good German and owned five farms — who offered $175. Besides the money, we would share some of the animals. For instance, there were twenty-four sows; we'd get two pigs a year from their litters to slaughter for meat. And we were able to earn some more money when the landlord got a second cow for us. We needed plenty of milk ourselves—Johanna had had another girl, Gerlyn, so we had six children by now. But we could separate the cream out from the milk and earn an extra $5 to $7 a week. The farmer's seven hundred chickens laid up to four or five hundred eggs a day which we sold at 30 cents a dozen, and we got half of that money, too. That's how we earned our grocery money. We also had a vegetable garden.

We were satisfied. And the nice thing was that we were all by ourselves. The owner lived in town and he'd check on us just a few times a week. Before, the landlord lived right there on the same place with us.

We stayed for a year and a half. Then we moved to a better place—partly because the house where we lived was so cold in the winter, and it didn't even have running water. We had to go and fill a pail outside at the well. But the big difference was that I was renting the new farm. I was no longer just a farm laborer. I was at least half-independent; whatever I earned over and above the rent would be mine.

I remember when the couple who were the owners checked us out to see if we'd be good renters. First thing, the lady went into the cellar to see what kind of wife I had. There she could see the jars and jars of preserved fruits and vegetables. Her husband went out into the farmyard with me and looked at everything. They wanted to know their farm and their money would be in good hands.

It was a big step for us; we hadn't been in America three years. But we had a good friend who helped us, and the retired couple who owned the farm were also willing to loan us money for machinery and other things to get started. We stayed there six years—and our seventh child, Arnold, was born there.

But I really wanted to be independent, to have my own farm. To reach that goal more quickly, I rented a second farm along with the first.

Then in 1959, seven years after coming to America, we found a 250-acre farm we could buy. It cost $40,000, but only $8,000 down payment. We've been here ever since—although we've enlarged the farm and improved the house, too. This house didn't have running water either, and it was really run–down. But we improved the farm first. A house earns no income!

How to Do It

We worked and worked and, for a long time, never took a vacation. The first one was in 1965, to visit Germany. That was thirteen years after we came to America. The farm was paid off, and our girls were married, but the boys were not old enough to need help starting on their own farms yet. The next vacation we took wasn't until seven years later. And only after twenty years in this country did we feel we could afford the time to go on vacation every other year.

But if I had to start farming over again, I wouldn't change much. It was the only way to start when you had nothing. And it worked; we made it.

You have to start with old equipment other people don't want. The first year, I bought an old tractor for $70, instead of spending $2,000 for a decent one. I bought an old wagon for $4; I figured it would last me the first year or two. The drag (harrow) cost $5 or $6. It was no good, but I figured I'd fix it up, straighten some old teeth up, and weld or bolt in some new teeth. And so it was usable for a few years. I put in my time to save money.

A cultivator came along with the $70 tractor. Then there was $20 for the disc. The corn planter I borrowed. I helped my neighbor put his corn in, and he let me use his planter. For the small-grain equipment (drill and combine) and for the corn picker, I worked in exchange for the use of the equipment.

If a farmer starting out today followed my way, he would save thousands and thousands of dollars. If he had to buy that simple equipment brand new, it would cost him $50,000, or maybe $70,000, plus interest. But I started out on $100 plus my labor. On that, I got my first crop into the corn crib.

All the equipment lasted at least one year, and it was paid for, too. So when I sold the crop—contracted it to the government—I was able to spend $500 or $600 more for a newer tractor, with an automatic starter; the old one just had a crank. I also got a plow and a cultivator and two different wagons. You

111

know, that old $5 drag actually lasted five or six years before I replaced it. Then, the third year, I bought a two-row corn planter. So it went, year by year.

We worked hard and we've done lots of things ourselves. We poured a lot of cement, for example, for all the floors in our buildings. They're not as nice as the ones when you hire a contractor, but they didn't cost any money. We always did as much work as we could ourselves.

We pulled ourselves up by our boot straps. We used to butcher chickens for people at 25 cents a head—the children remember helping with that. I baled hay for other farmers at $1 per hour. We always said, "A dollar earned when you don't have a dollar, or when you have to borrow it, is worth two dollars."

A neighbor who grew up here, a good friend, helped us get started. One time he suggested, "Let's go to the fair; it's the biggest fair around."

"Okay, we'll eat a sandwich before we go." But when I looked, there was no meat and no bread in the house.

He laid $10 down on the table, "Here, let me give you something." I paid him back in a couple of weeks, but that's the way it was. In the fall, before the crops came in, it was tough.

When we came to America, we came with almost nothing. After we got to Iowa, I went to the bank with my sponsor and signed a note for $600 to pay for the train trip from New York City and for some new clothes he wanted us to get. I was worried; I was responsible for my wife and five children, and I was going into debt. I told my sponsor, " This is the first debt I ever had in my whole life."

"In this country, if you want to make progress, you have to work with someone else's money." He told me the truth.

Three years later when we started on our rented farm, we had only about $1,000 in savings, and we had six children by then. So we had to borrow another thousand from our landlady and a thousand more from a friend who helped us so much. At that time, we hadn't established our credit, but the landlady and her three brothers owned the bank. That's how we could get a loan from her.

In the first year, we paid her back, plus paying off our seven heifers. But we wanted to buy a tractor and wagon, so we went back to her, and she loaned us money again. Then, next year we paid off that loan and borrowed again for more equipment and animals and other things, and so on. We never let the notes go overdue so we would lose credit, or at least we let them know if there would be a delay in paying them off. Sometimes we had to do that, if our crops were late.

So those are the secrets of our success. First, being healthy. Then you have to keep everybody busy. And we didn't spend money to do certain things, like going on trips or to shows. About the only movie shows we've seen are a few religious ones. We didn't go to dances. After we lost two farms, we said, "A dance means being happy, and we can't be."

Chapter 10

Surviving as a Farmer Today

The American family farm is increasingly in trouble. Farms have to get bigger and bigger just to survive. Many small farmers have had to sell out. The yeoman farmer that Jefferson saw as the backbone of our society is vanishing. In this chapter, Immanuel tells how his values form the way he and his sons run their family farms in order to survive.

Immanuel takes a conservative, and a conservation-minded, attitude toward farming. Farming in Swabia over the centuries had a survival orientation, a long-run view. The peasant husbanded resources and slowly built up the farm so future generations would have a livelihood. Children had no alternative work opportunities. There were no big cities with other kinds of jobs available.

Swabians ensured survival of the family farm by avoiding specialization; they wouldn't put all their eggs in the same basket. They preferred the security of mixed farming, raising a variety of crops and animals together. Calamities might strike several, but a few would be successful enough to ensure survival.

We have already mentioned the Swabian emphasis on frugality — waste is sinful. Mixed farming avoided waste by creating complementary and synergistic combinations. The wastes from one crop were often benefits for another, and vice versa. Swabian farmers, for example, would keep beehives. The bees made use of blossom nectar that would ordinarily be wasted. The farmer got honey out of that, and the fruit trees and other crops benefited from the pollination and setting of good crops.

Similarly, the farmer kept geese which ate the weeds growing underneath the fruit trees, while at the same time fertilizing the trees, in addition to producing goose eggs, meat, and featherbeds. Cows ate hay from land which could not be used for cultivation. They produced milk, as well as manure for the farmer's wheat, which in turn provided grain for the farmer as well as straw for the cows' bedding, and so on. The Swabian farm was a closed system in which little was wasted. The externalities of modern, specialized farming, such as pollution from chemical fertilizers and pesticides, were absent.

The small size of the Swabian peasant holdings — because they were usually divided among the children — also affected traditional agricultural practices, and, over time, the character of the people. A small farm forced the Swabian peasant to farm intensively — keep busy all the time and use his mind, since his land and physical capital were limited. It was no wonder that the Swabian peasant came to have the reputation of being "clever," which is to say, always thinking, attacking problems, and looking for a more efficient way. The Swabian farmer, through necessity, came to prefer a hands-on style of work, not setting up plans and routines at a distance, like a plantation farmer or factory manager.

Finally, the small, independent Swabian holdings also fostered initiative. The peasants were working for themselves. Each family member could affect the success of the farm. When someone has a stake in the enterprise like this, he or she will use initiative to seek out problems and apply the very best judgments in solving them. Such a farmer will also make efforts to learn from past experience, from the constant changes in animals, and nature, and markets. Because the Swabian farms were small, the peasants were forced to work "smarter," and because the farms belonged to them, they wanted to work "smarter."

As I see it, the farmer today has to be a businessman, a mechanic, a veterinarian — lots of things all at once.

The farmer is running a business, and he has to know how to manage his help. Each of my sons has a hired man to milk and feed the cows and help with the field work (planting, harvesting, haying) because that's where most of the feed for the cows comes from. We pay them a share of the milk check, so we don't have to supervise them all the time. In the last few years, this kind of hired help has become more and more common, as farms are getting bigger and bigger. But you have to give your hired men an incentive to work. The Russians don't produce enough food on their state farms for that reason. If they gave the land back to the farmers, they'd have enough food.

Our hired men all come from around here. They're usually in their twenties, and they all have a farm background. You try to keep hired men as long as you can, but you can't blame them if they quit and want to start on their own. When I started working for a farmer, he asked my plans. "I want to learn how to work the machinery, plus I need to get the money, but then I'm going to start for myself." And I did. But some like to work for somebody else; they don't want so much responsibility. There are different kinds of people, and you have to know how to manage each kind.

You might not think the mechanic part of being a farmer is important, but it is. Not everybody can do it. You have to learn how to take the equipment apart to get at what's giving you trouble. As you take it apart, you learn how it works and how it fits together. You figure out the part that's not working right and you replace it. In school, they don't have all the different machines. You have to learn how to figure things out yourself. And sometimes, it's not easy. You pinch your fingers, you skin your knuckles. But you get it done.

By taking the time to learn about and fix your equipment, you save lots of money on repair calls. You also save money because that lets you buy second-hand equipment instead of new. And you save on downtime. For example, when I cracked a wheel, I went and got the parts and fixed it myself. If you send for somebody, they spend at least half a day coming out to fix it. That half day costs me at least $100 in my own lost work time.

The farmer also has to be a veterinarian. Like yesterday, I had to give a calf a shot for pneumonia. I could see it in the eyes and ears and how it acted. The calf drank only half its milk. And normally a calf's ears are up and the eyes are wide open, bright and shiny. But this one wasn't well. The ears were bent a little, they folded back, and the eyes were closed a little and blurred over. Right away when I notice that, I will give it a pill. And if it doesn't get well after that, I'll give it a shot.

Strategies for Survival

We like to raise different animals here. I like chickens. We used to have five or six hundred laying hens, but now you need tens of thousands of hens and your own egg packing plant if you're going to make money. So we just keep enough chickens to supply our own eggs. They're always fresh and taste good, and I know everything the chickens ate.

My son Arnold likes hogs. Sometimes he has six or eight hundred of them. Right now pigs are down in price, so he doesn't raise many. I used to raise pigs until my sons got their own farms. Then it got too hard to do pigs besides the milking and the crops. And on top of all the extra work, with pigs you have to watch them closely; there are so many sicknesses. But the advantage to pigs is that they're quick—only five to six months to raise a pig compared to two years for a heifer or a steer.

What it boils down to, it's hard to do pigs, milk, crops, and beef all together. There's too much work. A lot of farmers go more and more into one line—milk only, pigs only, or farm crops only. The other advantage to that is you don't have to have all those different kinds of machinery for each animal or crop.

Of course, milk gives you the best income if you don't mind all the labor. And the cash is steady. Every two weeks you get a milk check. But to expand at milking, you have to buy more and more land until you can't handle it. You need to raise most of your own feed. If you have to buy a lot, it won't work. Besides, we don't like to do just milking either.

We like variety. For example, we've been feeding beef cattle for about ten years. We raised fifty head from our own stock. They're fed silage and fermented grain. That way we don't have to buy much protein supplement.

Another thing, we enjoy working outside. It's boring if you're only in the barn with the livestock. Crops plus livestock give you different types of work through the day.

We grow mainly corn. This year we also grew forty acres of soybeans, but they loosen the ground, so when it rains, the soil runs off where it's hilly. That's why we don't like to plant beans.

The first thing with corn is picking out the right varieties to grow. It can make ten to fifteen bushels (up to 10 percent) difference in your yield. In late winter, each seed company has meetings where they give out booklets that tell you this and that farm grew these varieties—there'll be fifty or one hundred farms. Then we look on the map for our area and growing season. Here it's 110 days maximum. So we look at varieties of corn that take, say, 100 to 110 days to ripen. There'll be three or four different varieties, and we pick out the highest producing variety, one that gives from 100 to maybe 130 or 150 bushels per acre.

You get the higher number of bushels when the heat is right—eighty to ninety degrees—and when there's enough rain and plenty of sunshine. Too hot and dry can mean 100 bushels or even less. The book will recommend two or three varieties at 110, 105, and 103 days and we'll pick from those, too. Maybe we'll also pick out a 95 day variety that doesn't yield as much but has better quality. Last year we had bad weather in the spring, so we changed to an earlier corn, one we could harvest more quickly. You try to work with the weather, if you can.

You have to find the right balance between crops and different animals. My son Erich doesn't raise pigs because his milking parlor milks a lot of cows, and he raises corn and hay. That keeps him busy enough. If corn is cheap, then you can buy it and feed some beef cattle, and maybe even a few pigs, too. What you do depends on prices, too.

But in general, we all milk and we raise corn, a varying number of pigs, and some chickens, too. Like in Bessarabia. We had a mixture there, too.

Some other farmers here specialize. Some might have more than a thousand pigs. Others might have only feeder cattle — maybe a thousand of them.

If I were forced to specialize, I'd specialize in milk. It's dependable. But if we had done only cows when starting out, I would have needed a job in town as backup for a long, long time. It's expensive to build up a herd. Of course, the real costs for a dairy farmer are in work, especially in the milking twice a day for 365 days a year. If you can do it, and you like that kind of work, you always come out better off than the average farmer.

We don't always earn money on everything. Milk, yes, but pigs only sometimes, and the same for beef, corn, and soybeans. If you have four of these things, you'll always survive. You've got to have more than one or two.

Security

People wonder why we buy certain big machines. For example, we have a big 260 horsepower, four-wheel drive Case tractor. It's used just four or five weeks in the spring, that's all. The real reason we have it is for security.

We use the Case for chisel plowing, a kind of minimum tillage. Instead of the soil getting turned over, the plow mainly chisels through it. With the big Case we can chisel fourteen feet across at once. To get a crop in, we use three different passes across the field. First, we chisel a foot deep and put anhydrous ammonia in. Then we disc it and level it, and that's in a twenty-five-foot wide swath with the Case. Finally, we go over with the planter, and at the same time put insecticide six inches on either side of the seed. It's a twelve-row planter, and we can cover 110 to 120 acres per day.

Having a big tractor means you can speed up all this work in getting the crop in. The earlier you put the seeds in, the better the crop, because there's more growing time. Sometimes, but seldom, we can plant in late April. If we have to wait till the fourth or fifth of May, then we have to push to get it in. After May tenth or fifteenth, we say, "It's one bushel less per acre for every day we can't plant." On a yield of a 100 to a 140 bushels per acre, that's close to 1 percent less for every day lost. You really start sweating when it rains a couple of weeks and the fields are too wet for you to finish your planting.

You also want to plant quickly to avoid possible problems with a late harvest. An early frost can catch the corn if it's still in the milk stage and prevent it from ripening further. The corn kernel is killed, it just stays soft. It'll rot instead of ripen.

In 1982, we had three weeks of rain during the normal planting time, and we didn't get some 800 acres planted till the beginning of June. In the fall, the corn stayed soft. It had too much moisture in the kernels. We were burning a thousand gallons of liquid propane gas a day to dry that corn. We had to, it was too late in the fall to let it dry out in the field. Then, on the eleventh of December, the propane dryer overheated with 4,000 bushels of corn in it. It caught fire and burned for over fifty hours. We lost both the dryer and the corn.

For corn to dry, it has to be continuously stirred around to let the hot air in to pick up the moisture. But the corn was too wet—it had close to 40 percent moisture, instead of a normal 27 or 28 percent. Probably the wetter corn didn't move up from the bottom of the drying bin, where the gas flames are. The heat made the wet corn swell, it jammed up and then it caught fire. The other drying bins, with corn that was planted in early May, were fine.

I'll never forget that day. The fire department couldn't get the corn to stop burning. They kept pumping water into the drying bin, but the water couldn't get down into the jammed-up corn. It just kept burning underneath. So they put on special clothes and masks and shoveled all the burning corn out by hand. We had to scatter it in the fields and let it burn itself out there.

That's why we like a big tractor. We can get the planting done quickly, even if the weather forces us to start late.

Proving Yourself—and Giving Lessons

Out here on the farm we had to prove ourselves to other people, to the neighbors. That's the way it is when you're new. You have to build your credit up—with the bank and also with other people; that's what we did.

When we first came to America, we didn't see many things; it was all too new. But later we saw how the farming was at a standstill until we immigrants came in. We had lost everything—our property, our home, our citizenship. So we were hungry. We wanted to get ahead. We were so many years without a home, and that's as low as you can sink in the world. We said, "If we ever have a chance to get our own place, we're going to do whatever it takes." I think the refugees gave the whole Western World a lift. In Germany, there were eleven million refugees—all working hard.

One thing we started here was terracing. Other people said we were spending our money foolishly, but they were still thinking in the old ways. We can't let good ground run away—the generation after us has to live, too.

We used to have bad washouts and waterways on the hilly fields around here. A terrace has a flatter slope, so you don't lose much soil. If there is any run-off water, it's gathered by a pipe which runs under the terraces. Water that doesn't soak into the terraces will drain into our woods.

We hired a bulldozer to cut and build-up the terraces according to the survey we had done. It was laid out so each terrace had about the same number of rows. Corn can survive under water up to five or six hours or more, and the first year it did. We had four inches of rain all at once, and you could see nothing but water on the terraces; it looked like a lake. I wondered whether the terraces were worth all that money, but the next day everything was okay. We saved thousands of dollars and tons of soil in just one day with those terraces. And our fertilizer didn't run off into the rivers, either.

We try to do a good job with what we already have, rather than expanding more and more. Many farmers are selling out now. It first began in the seventies, then more so in the last four or five years. They started out too big, with a big new barn and many milk cows. With the land, the farm machinery, cows, and so on, together it cost them from $300,000 to $500,000 to start. And they kept getting bigger, with interest up to 19 percent. I told the boys it was better to pay rent, say $100 an acre, even if you could buy land cheap, like $1,000 at 10 percent. So we agreed. For a while we just rent instead of expanding more. We just make sure we survive. And we do.

Chapter 11

The Next Generation

America *is a relatively tolerant and open society. New people, with new ways, can usually fit in without too much trouble. But small-town and rural America is more traditional and less forgiving to those who are different.*

It helped that Immanuel and Johanna's neighbors had the same farming background as they did. Researchers have shown that people with a farm or a rural background generally have a stronger work ethic than those growing up in a city. The latter are more likely to do just the work defined as necessary to earn their pay, while the former believe in doing a good job as defined by the work, not by the boss or the pay.

But Immanuel and Johanna and their children differed from their neighbors because they were immigrants. They had a double dose of the work ethic. They had the enormous drive to work and get ahead which most American immigrants have. Researchers have compared the work ethic of school children at differing removes from the immigrant experience—school children who came as immigrants, those whose parents were immigrants, and those whose grandparents were the immigrants. The closer the children were to the immigrant experience, the harder they worked at their studies.

Immanuel and his family had an additional adjustment problem specific to the twentieth century. People of German origin have had to cope with the hatred of people whose countries were attacked by the Germans in two world wars.

Our Boys Were Fed Up With School

When they were growing up, I told the boys, "You have a choice — we'll help you go to college, or you can get a loan and we'll help you get started farming." College would have cost them less, but they wanted to start farming.

Erich and Sig were both fed up with school. Kids on the school buses picked on them because they were new and because they were German. Real roughness is not allowed on a bus, but when they got off there was lots of trouble. I remember even Gerlyn came home one day and said, "They threw an apple core at me." So the children felt they were not liked by others at school.

When Erich belonged to the Future Farmers of America in high school, they visited our farm. We had a Massey-Harris tractor, and a boy said, "What kind of junky tractor is that?" The boy didn't even have one this size. He just said it to show off, to put Erich down in front of the others.

The problems had a lot to do with the children's ages. The ones who were younger when we first came here were all right. Arnie just started the first grade so he had no real problems; he grew up with the others. But Gerlyn was ten or eleven when she started school here, when they threw the food at her.

But all the boys were happier if they could be on the tractors. They started when they were ready to work the clutch. They couldn't sit; they could only reach it standing up. They were about seven or eight years old. The first work they did with the tractor was raking hay. It's slow, and it's not dangerous work. The boys like to tell people, "We got started by going out in the barn, because that's what our father did."

Conflicts

I know what my kids went through; I still have problems here when I say my name with my German accent. There are problems with younger people, too, not older people. Some in town just don't want to understand.

Now there is a mixed feeling. It used to be worse. It had to do with the war, of course. All the bad things came out in the newspaper here. And they have relatives over there, they go back and hear things from them.

Some of them here are nice, some not. After we were here ten years, one man still said to us, "If these kind of people don't behave, send them back." He meant us! But we get along fine with his neighbors. It just depends on the person.

Of course, we had conflict in Bessarabia, too. Our village there was pretty big, with four different sections. If you wanted to visit a girl in another section, you had to give the boys an *Eimer*, a pail of wine. That was no big deal since every farmer had a vineyard and plenty of wine. And you had to do that only once, to get the right to visit in another section. But if you didn't, you would have to get your friends to fight. And boys could be almost killed fighting over a girl because they used clubs and iron rods.

There were seven *Elternmänner* (elders) responsible for keeping peace in the village, one for each night of the week. By ten o'clock there had to be peace. If you did anything — played an accordion, sang, anything — they had rubber clubs. They said, "Boys, time to go home," and they'd beat the heck out of you. Or they could put you in jail. If you were quiet, you could stay out all night or go to someone's home if you wanted — the wine was free everywhere since everybody raised so much.

What you didn't do was travel much to other villages. They were maybe five miles apart. Since we didn't have any cars, each village was almost like a separate world.

You normally stayed pretty close to the family quarters until you were fourteen or fifteen years old — when you were confirmed. Before that, you were considered a kid; you had schoolwork to do at home and no free time. Afterwards, you were an adult, and you had to join a group. You could sing together with the other boys, and you would start seeing girls.

But there were no girls on the street. A girl who stayed out would be considered a tramp. A girl was something special. Girls had to do housework and crocheting and sewing; they had to prepare their dowries, and they made everything by hand, even the sheets. I still have the suit my sister made for me from our own sheep's wool. She did it instead of my mother, because my mother died when I was thirteen.

When people went visiting, the women would take *"Trumpf"* along — their knitting or crocheting, or even their spinning wheel. They didn't take patching or mending — only new stuff they were making. A woman always had work to do—there wasn't any card playing by them.

Johanna interjects:

That's the way it still is for me here; I'm always busy. I have five or six men around—my husband and also my sons and the hired men if they're working here. So I cook for them, I wash clothes for them, I do patching and sewing, and I work in the garden. To relax, I crochet things for the church and for presents. I don't watch TV except for the news. When I sit down, I fall asleep.

In Bessarabia we were always working on some kind of housework. When I came here to America, I didn't think I could ever sit and not do something—except for Sunday, our day of rest.

Immanuel again:

Here some women are different. My two youngest boys—they're in their early thirties—didn't get married for some time. Who wants to marry a farmer here? The girls will work—do the farm books and do the housework, and maybe run the tractor sometimes or feed the cows. But there are limits. Some ladies don't understand. On a farm, the work comes first and the pleasure second. In the spring and in the fall, there are weeks when the farmer has absolutely no free time. He works till midnight. Some wives want to live <u>now</u>. By six o'clock, a husband is supposed to come home, clean up, and sit down for dinner. Our boys couldn't do that when they were starting out, and the girls here couldn't understand it. But the boys are lucky now. They found some girls who understand what it means to be a farmer.

Inheritance in Bessarabia

The practice in Bessarabia was for all the boys to inherit the land. The parents would split up the farm, so farms would get to be scattered pieces like in Schwaben.

The girls usually didn't inherit land. I had two brothers and three sisters, but only we three boys got land. We had to pay our three sisters money as their share of the inheritance. Sometimes girls would get some land, like Johanna did. Her father had a big farm, almost two hundred acres, and there was only one son. So he got maybe eighty acres and each of the three girls also got some land, forty acres apiece.

That would be a big help to a girl, to inherit land. In courting, the boys looked at the girl and also at what she would get. The boys all knew how much land the parents had.

When a boy over there married, he got a team of horses and a wagon, a cow or two, and maybe five or ten sheep. It was called an *Aussteuer* (dowery) and it helped him start farming. The land the boy was to inherit was given to him then, except the father would keep a few acres back, which the boy would farm for him. That's the way it was in my family. My father kept five acres back from each of us three boys, and we worked them for him.

A boy was able to get married when he wanted. His parents, if they saw she was a good girl, would say, "Go ahead." Some parents really hurt themselves. They might become poor by passing on the farm to the boy. But that's the way it was done.

The parents stayed on the homestead for the rest of their lives. They would have a separate kitchen, living room, and bedroom all to themselves. If the house wasn't big enough for that, then the children built them a separate one. The idea was that they be nearby so their children could care for them. This was automatically understood by all. Most families—parents, grandparents, and children got along so well with each other that you really couldn't think of it being otherwise.

I was still young at the time I saw all this, and it could be there were times when not all went smoothly. But we just couldn't visualize any other way. We honored our parents and grandparents. We were grateful to be able to care for them.

That was before television and other outside influences. Even the radio was rare. Children were mostly influenced by their home life and by the school and church. Everywhere they were taught, "Honor your father and mother—so that you may live upon this earth both well and long."

And that's what the world is missing today. Children don't learn it anymore. So today we have robbers and murderers. We have fraud and deceit, and we have sex for breakfast, sex for midday, sex for evenings—sex day and night. God can no more bless us Christians than the godless communists. We had better do something before it's too late!

I should mention another thing we had in Bessarabia—honesty. By law, there had to be a written contract when people bought a horse or cow, so people could know it wasn't stolen. But people used to speak of "the German's word." If you made a deal, all you needed was a handshake, you didn't exchange the ownership papers and money right away. You'd say, "Let's have a *Mogaritsch*," a glass of wine or whiskey. If you promised to sell an animal for a certain price, a German's word meant everything, and the other nationalities believed them. Oh, we had a few who didn't keep their word, but almost everybody did. A German's pride meant more to him than money. If he gave his word, he would keep to the deal, even if somebody else offered him more money.

Our Children

Only two of our sons wanted to be farmers, and we helped with some of the land and some of the livestock. The third one studied to be a mechanic, but he eventually came around, too.

Our three older girls—well, we weren't able to help them because we had nothing then. In fact, when we bought our farm, we borrowed some money for the down payment from them, as well as from the bank.

Erna was a director for Mary Kay Cosmetics supervising fifty to a hundred saleswomen. She now works for the Defense Department like her husband.

Hilma has an office job. She married a guy who worked for a finance company, and he worked as a salesman awhile, but later they went into farming for a time, too.

Gerda's the only one of the girls still in farming. She never wanted to be a farmer's wife. She saw the life her parents lived. "It's such hard work," she said. "You can't go to a show or to a restaurant or go on vacation. Why should I want to live a life like this?" Then she came home with a boy who was a farmer. She said she changed her mind. They're big farmers now, with one thousand acres out in western Iowa. They do it all by themselves. They have twice as much land as farmers around here.

Our fourth daughter, Gerlyn, went to college, and we helped her do that. We didn't take any government help. She's an administrator for a nursing home with eighty people now, and her husband has a good job, too.

It makes you think, though. In Bessarabia, almost all of the children went into farming. Here, only half of ours — and for some other families, no one. My brother made a study of what happened to the thousands of Bessarabians who settled in Germany. Only a single one got to be an independent farmer. You have to wonder, is that a good thing?

The Good Farmer Has Mental Discipline

It takes more than just good land and hard work to make a success of farming. There are some young men who are good people and hard workers, too, but they can't last. They lose everything because they don't have the ability to manage themselves. They can't make the decisions when they have to, and that's what farming's about. They have to be told what to do.

As a farmer, you have to know what's important. You have to know what has to be done when. You live with Mother Nature, and you make decisions accordingly. For example, you can't make hay when the hay gets too old. When alfalfa starts blossoming, or even before, it's the best. Later, it has less protein. So when the time is right, that hay has to be your top priority.

You have decisions with animals, too. You have to handle a milk cow right; and the better she is handled, the more milk she will give. Good feed is the most important requirement, and next, dry bedding for sleeping on.

A cow, like every animal, has feelings just like humans. Whoever treats us nice, we are nice to in turn. If they bully us, we try to ignore them. Milking, for example, has to be done with the right touch, the udder washed with warm water, and the teats slowly prepared with a hand massage. After the milk machine has been on the cow for some two or three minutes, you'd have to check to be sure she isn't milked out. If she is, you have to take the machine right off. You can ruin a cow by milking too long. She can get an infection easily and even lose her udder. And, it's mostly the very best milk cows that need the most attention and best handling. They're the ones that are the most delicate.

The farmer has to be thinking all the time. Once in western Iowa, while I was going out to do the morning milking, a neighbor drove by on the way home from a dance. I said to myself, "He won't be one hundred percent when he's working today." Your mind has to be there one hundred percent or else you'll make mistakes — you could have an accident.

For example, when you cultivate corn for eight or twelve hours a day, it's easy to take your eyes away from the rows for a second. Then you'll dig some of the corn plants out or cover them up with too much dirt. Either way, the plants are dead, and you lose a quarter to half a pound of corn for each plant you destroy. And you can destroy a lot of plants real quickly when your cultivator is working eight or twelve rows at the same time.

So you have to watch yourself. I found it was best for me to stop every two or three hours. I'd drink a cup of coffee and then lie flat on the ground with my eyes closed. After five minutes of that, I can do a better job.

You always have to be thinking about what you're doing — and also what you're going to do next. Machines can go on operating even if you're not thinking for them. Your mind has to be there. On some jobs, you can daydream, but not on the farm. It's easy to ruin your machinery on the farm.

Even after years and years of farming, I make mistakes. But, of course, I'm getting old. The other day I was mowing and I forgot there was a stump right outside the edge of a field, twelve inches away. It was a $3,000 machine, and the repair cost over $1,000. Well, the machine was insured, but there was still the loss of time. I lost that whole day of work.

Another example — the hired man didn't notice a different noise from the tractor, and he broke a big casting. Years ago, when the horses were tired, they stopped on their own. Or they kicked you. But now, there are no horses to tell you when to stop.

So today it's especially hard for young people — they have to have all kinds of knowledge, as well as working hard and being good managers. In Bessarabia, the work was harder on your body. You had to do things like picking corn by hand or cutting hay with the scythe. But you could daydream. We used to say, "To work with the scythe you need a strong back and a weak mind." But even in Bessarabia, you also had to be a good manager to get ahead.

Chapter 12

German Success Breeds Hatred

G*ermans have left their lands to seek a better life for centuries, as far back as the Middle Ages when there was organized colonization of the sparsely settled lands east of the Elbe River. In recent centuries, peasants from overpopulated southern Germany responded to invitations from various rulers in Austria-Hungary or Russia. They often filled the mostly empty borderlands reconquered from the Turks, as was the case with the Bessarabian Germans. In addition, the rulers hoped the German peasants would serve as models for their own peasants who farmed according to feudal traditions.*

The Germans came as free peasants and were treated as such by the nobles who invited them. Naturally the peasants had to pay taxes, but they did not have to perform personal duties for the rulers, as did the local peasants. So there was often a major difference between the Germans as independent peasants — motivated by personal initiative — and the Eastern European peasants who were mostly either day laborers or serfs for their ruling nobility — their individual initiative stifled. Immanuel describes the difference:

We had a story in Bessarabia: One morning a Bulgarian, a Romanian, a Turk, and a German were told all the land they could pace off by the end of the day would be theirs. After an hour, the Romanian decided to stop, sit down, and eat breakfast. The Bulgarian didn't stop till his midday meal. The Turk stopped in the evening, at supper, "Anyway, that's all I need," he said. But the German kept going and going. He was finally so exhausted, he just fell down. But as he fell, he stretched out his hand as far as he could reach, "Up to here is mine." Then he died!

Hatred in Bessarabia

It seems that in each country there are some who are hated. The Germans were hated well before Hitler. Even in the Tsar's time. Other people saw the Germans were so successful, and they said, "Why can't our people have it good, too? We have to get rid of these Germans!"

The Germans were invited by the Russian government, but it just made for hatred. Some of the others — the Bulgarians and Russians — ended up working for the Germans.

Germans were deported to Siberia by the Russians in 1915, during World War I. The Russians were afraid they might sympathize with the German government. The border between Russia and Romania was along the Prut River then, west of us — and the Russians started to deport Germans who lived within 150 kilometers (90 miles) of the border, all along the Prut, up to Volhynia.

Our parents had the horses and wagon ready but were saved by a snowstorm. A railroad went through our area, and the people were put to work keeping the snow cleared away. In the meantime, a Russian official who liked the Germans traveled up to the Tsar and arranged it so we could stay, even though we lived near the border. But the Volhynian Germans weren't that lucky.

After Bessarabia became Romanian, we still saw some of the same hatred. At first, there were few Romanians around, but after 1918, it changed. For me, the hatred was mostly in the military — mostly from the ordinary soldiers who thought we were followers of Hitler. The officers, I have to say, at least in our unit, treated Germans okay. But in other units, there were also some officers who really mistreated the German recruits. They made them their personal servants.

134

Hatred in America

Some things in America aren't too different from over there. The local people have been here so long, and then they see us come along, and we're successful. They don't like it. Like when I happened to drive by a sale near my farm, and I bid on the land and got it. Afterwards, I was told that another guy at the sale would have bid up the price just to keep me from getting it. But I was lucky, he didn't recognize me.

They're not all that way, I get along with most everybody. And the ones who say something about Germans, I don't challenge them. Otherwise the feelings will get worse.

We had plenty of trouble earlier. In 1968, Erich and I each borrowed $15,000 to build a milking parlor and a silo and to make other improvements. That was a lot of money then.

A year after we expanded, somehow a bug got into the cows and showed up in the milk. The creamery told us, "We can't take your milk as drinking milk, as Grade A. It has to go as Grade B. You have to check each cow, each quarter (teat) until you find where the bug is." See, if a cow has mastitis, an inflammation in the teats, you have to check each of your sixty cows and each quarter of the udder. That's 240 teats where the infection could be.

The milk is still okay for cheese and other things where they heat it real high. But when they mark down milk from Grade A to Grade B, you lose 50 cents to $1 per 100 pounds. When you're producing 2,000 pounds of milk, that's $10 or $20 per day you're losing, and we had borrowed a lot of money.

We eventually found which cow it was and treated her with medicine. Normally, the healing would take one to two weeks — four weeks at the most. But even after that, they didn't put us on Grade A again. After three whole months, we started to think. We had our suspicions.

An infection in the cows can happen to anybody, but the difference with us was that they didn't put us back on Grade A again. The field man said we were the ones who had to prove the milk was okay again. So we took samples from the same tank of milk that we gave to our creamery and sent them to three other creameries. They said, "Negative, no problem." But our creamery said we still had the same bug in the milk.

135

So we called one of the three creameries, even though it was across the state line, in Minnesota, and asked if they would take our milk. "Yes, yes." So we switched.

When we told our old creamery, they called their headquarters and got in touch with the state inspector. They told him we were selling Grade B milk as Grade A. He said according to the law, only our original creamery—the one that took us off Grade A—can put us back onto Grade A. So the local creamery then called and told our new creamery that they didn't have the right to put us back on Grade A.

Well, we didn't know about the law, and we were really worried. But it turned out okay, because the law in Minnesota is that you can take your milk to anyone. You don't have to go back to your old creamery first to be regraded.

Our old creamery didn't like it at all when they lost our business. The field man also was losing money when we switched to a new creamery and so was the milk hauler. We were right on his pickup route and he had to pass us by. They asked us why we didn't come back.

I told them off. I should have said nothing. But when you're angry, what can you do?

We deal with them again today. A larger company bought them out, so we went back. These people who gave us a hard time couldn't accept other people doing things in a new way. You see, twenty years ago we had the first modern milking parlor and also a silo with an automatic loader and feeder. We also put up a barn with over a hundred free stalls, and we were proud.

Yes, we really made waves, and people wondered how we could do it. They said, "How can they do this? Probably they get money from Germany!"

When we were in western Iowa, people said we got a start because the church gave us $2,000. I told them, "If you believe that, you go see the pastor. You know him. You ask him for the same, and you'll get it—zero!"

Today there are still some people who believe we visit Germany to get money. At first, we were pretty upset about that kind of talk, but you really can't stop it. Now, if we hear someone still saying that, we just have to laugh: "Why doesn't he go back to his own country and get some money, too?"

Chapter 13

Visiting The Communists

We tried to visit our old home in Bessarabia — we made arrangements while we were on a three-week tour of Romania. First we went to the Russian Embassy in Bucharest; we walked up to this great big building. Our hearts were really pounding. Past two soldiers, into the entrance where there was a big room with chairs, we waited and waited. We could hear someone typing, but we couldn't figure out which door goes where. We saw no signs. We thought maybe they were watching us first to see what we would say. Finally Johanna couldn't stand it anymore: "I'm leaving — with you, or without you." So we left.

In the U.S. we got a warning sheet about going behind the Iron Curtain: "Take no written or typed materials, no books; and Obey orders." That's why we were so very careful.

Instead, we went to the Romanian tourist agency in Bucharest. We arranged a car and a driver and so on, all kinds of things for a visit to Bessarabia. Because the Romanian phone system was no good, the tourist official would get cut off a lot. She was very efficient — she spoke German, but our tour bus had to leave by 10 a.m., and we really wanted to make all the arrangements for this visit to our Bessarabian home. So we missed the bus, and the phone bill cost $100. But we had everything set, everything but the permission from the Russians. We had seven days to get their answer.

Some time later we heard from Moscow, "No, it's a restricted area." The Romanian tourist agent told us, "They closed the door on you because you are from America — but you are really Romanian, you were born here. Those Russians, they stole our land; they stole Bessarabia."

All our work setting up the trip was for nothing, but we didn't know that at the time. When we rushed back to the tour buses, they were gone — to where, we didn't know. Back at the tourist office, they finally found out where the buses were supposed to be at midday, so we rushed to catch a train.

Our hotel was just a block from the train station in Bucharest, so we lugged our heavy suitcases there ourselves. As we came around the corner, a porter saw us. He knew we were foreigners from our clothes, and came up to us right away.

"Where are you going?"

"Ploesti."

"Quick, the train leaves in just a few minutes." And he took our suitcase and went right past all the people and up to the ticket window. He pushed everyone aside.

"Two tickets to Ploesti. These people are from abroad and have to be there by noon."

So people gave way, and he got our tickets for us. We were only inside the train two or three minutes before it left.

The Bastards Stole Our Lands

The people in our train compartment could see we were foreigners, and a man asked, "How do you know Romanian?"

"We're from Bessarabia."

"You are one of us!"

He was a Romanian who had fought in the war, south of Stalingrad. He was a mechanic — one of the highest paid jobs in Romania. He made 1,700 *lei* a month, but, poor guy, it took him a half or more of that just to buy a suit. We talked about the Russians: "Them bastards, they stole our land, they stole Bessarabia," he kept saying.

The other man and woman in the compartment also complained about the Russians. It was an interesting conversation. But we were very careful about what we said — we didn't want to get in trouble. In Eastern Europe people really can't trust each other.

At Ploesti we went to the restaurant where our tour was supposed to eat dinner. But no tour. We were sent to another restaurant. They said they didn't know anything either. But when they heard we were Bessarabians, they were nice and explained that the tour had canceled the meal. We wondered, maybe the tour guide changed the route so that they would lose us.

We finally were able to call Bucharest and learn the town where they would spend the night. When we got to the hotel, a modern and expensive hotel just for foreigners, they said they didn't know anything about the tour. But they would be happy to rent us a room at their awful prices. Well, we decided to wait at the restaurant and, sure enough, the tour buses finally came.

Then we had an experience at the hotel. A professor's wife travelling on the tour asked a hotel worker—she must have asked in German—for information on how to visit a church. Later, at two in the morning, we were awakened by noises, and when we looked out the window, we could see someone being beaten.

The next day, as we left, we saw that worker again, and we could see she had been the one who was beaten. I think they punished her because they don't want their people to have contacts with foreigners. This professor's lady asked us to speak to the woman in Romanian. I told the lady to look around because there was a man with dark glasses watching us.

"If I talk to her, they'll beat her worse. She has to live here, we don't."

Learning Some Lessons

Then we travelled over the mountains to Kronstadt (Brasov). We had college students travelling with us on the tour, and they started throwing their frisbees around the square. Romanians came and watched, and the students showed some teenagers how to play. More and more people crowded around to watch.

Three taxis were waiting at a taxi stand, and a frisbee flew right in the open window of one. An American student tried to get it. The taxi driver told him in Romanian, "Everything in this car belongs to me." The American didn't understand, so he just pushed the driver away and got the frisbee.

A few minutes later, we heard a siren coming closer and closer. A police car came up to us, right through the crowd. The police got out, grabbed a Romanian boy who had a frisbee in his hand, and took him away. When we looked around, we saw that the whole crowd had disappeared, just like that. Our students just looked at each other.

139

I guess the authorities didn't want the people to see too much or hear too much. The police ended it simply by taking one of them away—as an example to the others.

The American students really got an education there. More Americans should go and find out about the communist countries firsthand—so they appreciate where they live now. Sure, we had some good times there, but mostly it wasn't pleasant to see how the communists treat their people.

People were really poor in Romania. You would go walking in the market, and they would poke you with their arms or elbows. There was no conversation; they'd just say, "Mark?" Then, if there was no answer, "Dollar?" "Lei?" They wanted to exchange their *lei* for foreign currency. We tried to avoid them; it was too dangerous for us.

Then we visited a town in the northern part of Romania, in the Carpathians. After we got settled in the hotel, we went out walking. A Romanian came over and asked for cigarettes, and I gave him one. Next, he told me he wanted to buy some. I told him, "I have none for sale." I just gave him the whole pack. "Anything else for sale?" It was getting dark and he pointed over to an alley where there were no lights, "Let's go up there."

Well, it was way too dark for me. I started walking back to the hotel with the Romanian guy following behind. Then I saw Johanna talking to a German-Romanian couple who lived there. Right away they told Johanna, *"Verschwinde*—disappear. He's dangerous." Never again will I go out alone in the dark over there!

Then I met another guy. He spoke German and knew I was a tourist. He told me he worked in a forest, and he said, "I would like a chain saw, and in exchange I give you syrup, seven or eight liters." Now, what was he thinking? What would I do with a big can of syrup! "I work near the Russian border, and I have a girlfriend who lives on the other side. I see her every two weeks." He was telling me that he gets across the border easily. He was trying to get me into something.

"Enough of this," I thought. This system makes people prey on other people.

We know a couple who both got out of Russia during the war. The wife comes from the *Krim* (Crimea), and she speaks *schwäbisch,* so her ancestors immigrated to Russia from

Schwaben, too. Neither husband nor wife says much about what life was like for them under the communists. They're scared something might happen to them again, even here in America.

Once she said how during the planting season, a man found some sunflower seeds lying on top of the ground. So he ate them. The foreman saw him: "Those are government property. I can kill you right on the spot. Those are government property!" The communists would rather let the birds eat the seeds or let them lie wasted.

We know another German-Russian couple — from the Caucasus. Every once in a while the horror comes out — they'll say something and there will be tears in their eyes.

Chapter 14

Bad Dreams

As *refugees from the madness between Hitler and Stalin, Immanuel and Johanna are happy to have found peace in America. Yet there is still a feeling of not being completely at ease. They worry about Americans' lack of concern for what is going on in the world today—and about the American preference in associating evil with just the German side of the conflict they survived.*

You know what bothers me? Everyone knows about Hitler, about the Nazis and the bad things that shouldn't have happened. They did happen, and it's over now. But when you teach about Nazis, you should teach about the communist side, too.

At least the Nazis left us alone some of the time. We could go to church. They did try to get people away from church; they scheduled meetings and other things on Sunday morning. But you still had a choice — the church was still open. You could join the Party or join the church. Some did decide for the church.

We had no choices in Bessarabia in 1940. There was no way we could be free under the communists. The only possibility we had was to take up the offer by Germany and Hitler. We knew what was happening across the border in Stalin's land. In Germany, we had the possibility of some freedom. We gave up our land and livelihood because of that possibility. If we had stayed in Bessarabia, we would have been sent to Siberia — the men for sure. When we got to Germany, we heard about the Jews being persecuted — but we didn't know that they were being killed. I believe ninety percent of the people who lived in Germany didn't know that the concentration camps were for killing people.

For sure, the Jewish people have suffered a lot. They've been driven all over the world. Most Americans don't know how bad it is to be driven from your home. We know. Two times.

But here in America we keep seeing films that make all Germans out to be Nazis. Why are we smeared as murderers? It was not all Germans, but the regime that wronged the Jewish people. All Germans still have to pay for it, we overseas Germans, too. We didn't vote for Hitler; we did our duty as the Romanian citizens we were. Even today the hatred against Germans still continues. People envy Germans and so they call them "Nazis."

Those who have done wrong should be punished for it. But let the German people finally have some peace — us overseas Germans, too. Germany admits it did wrong and paid $600 million to Israel and $4 billion dollars to Jews under the restitution law, but where are the reparations from the Soviet Union for the wrong done us? Why do some people point at only one of the wrong parties?

We saw firsthand what the communists were like when they ran the government in Bessarabia in 1940. People who had thoughts along democratic lines disappeared. Then people who had been officers in the Tsar's army disappeared. Lots of people disappeared, and it didn't end after we left.

My friend from the Romanian army, Casier Nickoly, came from a wealthy Bulgarian family, and I wrote him in 1941 to find out how he was doing. Eventually I heard from his brother that Nickoly, his wife, and his parents, too, had all had been taken away by the N.K.V.D., the Soviet secret police. All the rich people, the politicians, the officers disappeared after the communists moved in.

When I talk about the choice between the Nazis and the communists, I suspect some people may not understand. Most people haven't experienced the two sides or they haven't wanted to be open to condemning both possibilities. Some people can see things only one way. That also happened in the Nazi times — some people in Germany were brainwashed. If people want to be just, they should listen to the evidence about the Nazis and the communists. Both.

Well, in Germany they tried and tried to make me become a member of the S.A. (*Sturmabteilung*) — an organization controlled by the Nazi Party. When we first arrived in Germany in 1940, they watched us closely. After all, we knew about democracy; the Nazis didn't run our villages in Bessarabia. Finally, in 1942, they wanted to take us into their organization. It was a hard for us; we were either for Nazis or against them. We wanted to take the middle way. We were religious and went to church and up to then had ignored the S.A. But I also knew roughly what could happen to me; after all, I was the only one still at home and only twenty-six years old. They had drafted people much older than I – thirty and older – and sent them to the front. They told me, "If you can't join us at the meetings, you're going to be sorry." That was in 1942, the war was three years old then.

The other thing, they brought account books out for me to keep records for the farm to report to them. I didn't want to. The farm was supposed to take the place of all we lost in Bessarabia. I felt, if I keep records and they pay me for that, I'd just be an administrator and part of the government. So I didn't.

"You're going to be sorry," they said. Sure enough, they drafted me in early 1943.

I turned to God. When I prayed, I asked only that we survive the war and come together again at home. The war went more and more downhill for Germany. It got harder and harder to think about what things would be like at the war's end. Would I live till tomorrow or the day after?

I prayed for Johanna and the three little children I had to leave at home. It helped each time when I was able to go on furlough and see they were all well. That's when I thought – and Johanna, too – that it was right to decide for church and not the Nazis.

I came out all right in the end. It turned out well, getting to America; and I guess I'm still pretty healthy, considering what I went through.

I've come to the end of my story. As in all beginnings, there must be an end. In these seven decades, we've had both nice days and dark days, days when we seemed to be at the edge of a bottomless pit, when we couldn't even think about any kind of a future.

But faith in God and in His guidance made a path for us. We were driven out of our Bessarabian homeland, but we thank

God that now in old age we can live in relative peace and freedom in the United States of America. For that, we give thanks every day.

Dreams

But sometimes I lie in bed and I still think about things, and it ruins the night. I thought about Grenada when the communists were in there — I thought how the Cubans didn't belong there! I think of Nicaragua now. And I think of all those countries that hate America.

I get excited and get into things. When I saw the college kids marching for peace, I told them, "Don't just stop at the courthouse. Go right on over to Moscow!"

If the communists do something — like when they killed the American major in East Germany — I think about it. I have dreams later.

It helps to talk with someone who understands — like other people from Eastern Europe who've lived under communism. You really have to experience it to know it. I'll tell some Americans about my experiences, but the next day they've forgotten what I told them. Maybe they feel that it doesn't matter.

Then there are those who like to talk politics, but they just can't visualize that the communists could have done these things to us. They think the communists are just friendly people like us. It makes me aggravated when these people feel they know better, even though they were never there living under the communists.

Sometimes my dreams wake me up, and I can't go back to sleep. The thoughts just keep on. One leads to the next, and on and on. I can't deal with it. So I get up, and do some work.

Bibliography

Bailey, Ronald H. Prisoners of War. World War II, Vol. 30. Alexandria: Time-Life, 1981.

Becker, Jakob. Bessarabien und sein Deutschtum. Bietigheim, Würrt.: Eduard Krug, 1966.

Bernard, William S. "Immigration: History of U.S. Policy" in Harvard Encyclopedia of American Ethnic Groups S. Thernstrom, ed. Cambridge: Belknap, 1980.

Berry, Wendell. A Continuous Harmony: Essays Cultural and Agricultural. N.Y.: Harcourt Brace Jovanovich, 1972.

Berry, Wendell. Home Economics. San Francisco: North Point, 1987.

Botting, Douglas. The Aftermath: Europe. World War II, Vol. 38. Alexandria: Time-Life, 1983.

Botting, Douglas. From the Ruins of the Reich: Germany 1945-1949. N.Y.: Crown, 1985.

Conquest, Robert. The Harvest of Sorrow: Soviet Collectivization and the Terror-Famine. N.Y.: Oxford Univ. Press, 1986.

de Zayas, Alfred M. Nemesis at Potsdam: The Anglo-Americans and the Expulsion of the Germans. London: Routledge & Kegan Paul, 1977.

Eberhardt, Elvire. "The Bessarabian German Dialect in Medicine Hat, Alberta." Doctoral Dissertation, University of Alberta, 1973.

Grosser, Alfred. Germany in Our Time: A Political History of the Postwar Years. N.Y.: Praeger, 1971.

Height, Joseph S. Homesteaders on the Steppe. Bismark: North Dakota Historical Society of Germans from Russia, 1975.

Height, Joseph S. Memories of the Black Sea Germans. np: Associated GR Sponsors, 1979.

Marrus, Michael R. The Unwanted: European Refugees in the Twentieth Century. N.Y.: Oxford Univ. Press, 1985.

Palmer, Alan. The Lands Between: A History of East-Central Europe since the Congress of Vienna. New York: Macmillan, 1970.

Read, Anthony and David Fisher. The Deadly Embrace: Hitler, Stalin and the Nazi-Soviet Pact, 1939-1941. London: Michael Joseph, 1988.

Rodefield, Richard D., et al. Eds. Change in Rural America: Causes, Consequences, and Alternatives. St.Louis: Mosby, 1978.
Ryder, A. J. Twentieth-Century Germany from Bismark to Brandt. N.Y.: Columbia University Press, 1973.
Schechtman, Joseph B. European Population Transfers, 1939-1945. N.Y.: Oxford University Press, 1946.
Schieder, Theodor, Ed. Dokumentation der Vertreibung der Deutschen aus Ost-Mitteleuropa: Vol. 1, Part 1, Die Vertreibung der deutschen Bevölkerung aus den Gebieten östlich der Oder-Neisse. Bonn: Bundesministerium für Vertriebene, 1954, and München: Deutscher Taschenbuch Verlag, 1984.
Schieder, Theodor, Ed. Dokumentation der Vertreibung der Deutschen aus Ost-Mitteleuropa: Vol. 4, Die Vertreibung der deutschen Bevölkerung aus der Tschechoslowakei. Bonn: Bundesministerium für Vertriebene, 1958, and München: Deutscher Taschenbuch Verlag, 1984.
Schieder, Theodor, Ed. The Expulsion of the German Population from the Territories East of the Oder-Neisse-Line. Bonn: Federal Ministry for Expellees, Refugees and War Victims, n.d.
Schieder, Theodor. Ed. The Expulsion of the German Population from Czechoslovakia. Bonn: Federal Ministry for Expellees, Refugees and War Victims, 1960.
Schieder, Theodore, Ed. The Fate of the Germans in Hungary. Bonn: Federal Ministry for Expellees, Refugees and War Victims, 1961.
Seton-Watson, Robert W. A History of the Roumanians from Roman Times to the Completion of Unity. 3rd ed., Hamden, Conn.: Archon Books, 1963.
Seton-Watson, Hugh. Eastern Europe Between the Wars, 1918-1941. 3rd ed., Hamden, Conn.: Archon Books, 1963.
Shafir, Michael. Romania: Politics, Economics and Society. Boulder, Colo.: Lynne Rienner Publisher, 1985.
Shover, John L. First Majority—Last Minority: The Transformation of Rural Life in America. De Kalb: Northern Illinois Univ. Press, 1976.
Simons, Gerald. Victory in Europe. World War II, Vol. 36. Alexandria: Time-Life, 1982.

Solzhenitsyn, Aleksandr. The Gulag Archipelago. Vol. 1. New York: Harper & Row, 1974.

Wagner, Immanuel. Zur Geschichte der Deutschen in Bessarabien. Stuttgart: Heimatmuseum der Deutschen in Bessarabien, 1958.

Weller, Karl and Arnold Weller. Würtembergische Geschichte im südwestdeutschen Raum. Stuttgart: Konrad Theiss, 1975.

Ziemke, Earl F. The Soviet Juggernaut. World War II, Vol. 25. Alexandria: Time-Life, 1980.

Ziemke, Earl F. Stalingrad to Berlin: The German Defeat in the East. Washington: U.S. Army. 1968.